The Bodhi Tree Grows in L.A.

D1053552

Also by Bhante Walpola Piyananda

Saffron Days in L.A.

Piyananda, Bhante Walpol
The bodhi tree grows in
L.A. : tales of a Buddhi
2008.
333305216060537
la   08/08/08

The Bodhi Tree Grows in L.A.

TALES OF A BUDDHIST MONK IN AMERICA

◆ ◆ ◆ ◆ ◆ ◆ ◆ ◆ ◆

Bhante Walpola Piyananda

◆ ◆ ◆ ◆ ◆

SHAMBHALA
Boston & London
2008

Shambhala Publications, Inc.
Horticultural Hall
300 Massachusetts Avenue
Boston, Massachusetts 02115
www.shambhala.com

© 2008 by Bhante Walpola Piyananda

All rights reserved. No part of this book may be reproduced in
any form or by any means, electronic or mechanical, including
photocopying, recording, or by any information storage and
retrieval system, without permission in writing
from the publisher.

9 8 7 6 5 4 3 2 1

First Edition

Printed in the United States of America

♾ This edition is printed on acid-free paper that meets the
American National Standards Institute z39.48 Standard.

Distributed in the United States by Random House, Inc.,
and in Canada by Random House of Canada Ltd

Library of Congress Cataloging-in-Publication Data
Piyananda, Bhante Walpola.
The bodhi tree grows in L.A.: tales of a Buddhist monk in
America / Bhante Walpola Piyananda.—1st ed.
p.   cm.
Includes bibliographical references.
ISBN-13 978-1-59030-568-3 (pbk.: alk. paper)
1. Buddhism—Anecdotes.
2. Piyananda, Bhante Walpola—Anecdotes. I. Title.
BQ4060.P58 2008
294.3'44—dc22
2007042740

To my students, past and present,
who have taught me more
than I've taught them.

CONTENTS

PREFACE

In 2001, my book *Saffron Days in L.A.* was published after months and months of writing and editing. I felt I had provided an enjoyable and accessible collection of Buddhist stories. I had combined my own direct experiences with traditional Buddhist teachings. As the book went to press, I hoped it would be of some value to Buddhists and other spiritual seekers.

Imagine my surprise when the book turned out to be a great success. Soon my publisher was encouraging me to put together a follow-up volume. I was humbled by the reception of the book and more than eager to comply in providing another series of accessible Buddhist teachings for readers. However, my other spiritual responsibilities, as abbot of my temple (Dharma Vijaya Buddhist Vihara of Los Angeles) as well as my responsibilities to various Buddhist organizations, took precedence and pushed back the writing of the second volume.

Finally, after a delay of a few of years, I was able to start assembling this second volume. I collected my thoughts and began organizing them, with the help of those thanked in the Acknowledgments to this book.

I struggled with thoughts of how to present these new stories. Should it just be more of the first book? Certainly its reception encouraged me to continue in the same vein. However, after a lot of thought, I determined to take this second book to another level.

So, while I hope the stories are just as entertaining and educational as in the previous book, the reader will find that the *Dhamma*, the Buddha's teachings, are explored in a bit more depth. Those who are familiar with Buddhism, and those who have read the first book, hopefully will find this a useful complement to deepen their understanding of the teachings of the Buddha.

For others of you, let me introduce myself. I am a monk of the Theravada tradition, the oldest of the three traditions, which has strived to preserve the original doctrines and practices taught by the Buddha 2,600 years ago. It is practiced mainly in Sri Lanka, Thailand, Burma, Laos, and Cambodia.

Mahayana is the next oldest tradition and it is practiced mainly in China, Korea, and Japan. Zen (or Chan) and Pure Land are two of the best-known schools in the Mahayana tradition. Vajrayana, the youngest of the three traditions, is practiced mainly in Tibet and the Dalai Lama is its most famous adherent. All three traditions follow the Buddha's teachings. The apparent differences are due to the varied cultures in which these traditions arose.

Theravada texts are preserved in Pali, a language that coexisted with Sanskrit from the Buddha's time. Pali and Sanskrit are similar but not identical; they are like two dialects of the same language. For example, the Sanskrit word *dharma* is rendered as *dhamma* in Pali, *karma* is *kamma* in Pali, *Nirvana* is *Nibbana*, and *sutra* is *sutta*. For your convenience, I have included a glossary at the end of the book.

The Buddha's teachings are straightforward, direct, honest, and open to all. However, it is easy to get caught up in the travails of daily living. We become so busy that we do not pause to see clearly how human life really works and what we can do to live more happily. My hope is that through these stories I can help readers achieve a greater insight into their own lives using the Buddha's teaching, so that they may have an even happier life for themselves and those around them.

May you be well and happy.

Bhante Walpola Piyananda
February 2007

ACKNOWLEDGMENTS

A book like this, while carrying the name of one author, is really a collaborative effort by many people. I have to thank first of all those people who appear in this book but whom I cannot name directly. I have been able to give a few real names, but in many instances I've had to protect the identities of the people I describe, and therefore I have changed their names and anecdotal details for the sake of confidentiality. Nevertheless, if they recognize themselves in these stories, I hope they will accept my deep thanks.

I would also like to express my deepest gratitude to those who helped me acquire the knowledge of Dhamma and experience in Buddhism. There are almost too many to name, but I would like to single out the following teachers: the late Ven. Walpola Nanaratana Thera, the late Ven. Balangoda Anandamaitreya Maha Nayake Thera, the late Ven. Dr. Kotagama Wachissara Thera, the late Ven. Dr. Havanpola Ratanasara Nayake Thera, the late Ven. Dr. Walpola Rahula Thera, the late Ven. Dr. K. Sri Dhammananda Nayake Thera, Ven. Lenagala Sumedhananda Maha Nayaka Thera, Ven. Dr. Kakkapalliye Anuruddha Nayake Thera, Ven. Dr. Henepola Gunaratana Nayake Thera, Ven. Weihene Pannaloka Nayaka Thera, Ven. Kurunagoda Piyatissa Nayake Thera, Ven. Madawela Punnaji Thera, Ven. Haupe Somananda Nayake Thera, Dr. Ananda Guruge, Kirthi Narampanawa, and Dr. George Bond.

In writing this book, I received invaluable help from Stephen Long (Bodhicari Dharmapala) and Ramya Gunasekara (Bodhicari Sanghamitta) who were largely responsible for the development of the first couple of drafts of the book. Their patient, tireless devotion to this project cannot be overestimated. Stan Levinson (Bodhicari Dharmajiva) helped with later copyediting and final organization of the material. Graciela Carabes, Carol Munday Lawrence, Ana Galvez Kadin, Susan Amarasekara, Lanka Ranasinghe (Bodhicari Khema), Raul Carabes, Sherry Cefali, Dr. Amali Jayasinghe, Dr. Claudia M. Vargas, Lokubanda Tillakaratne, Fredi Senaviratne, Dr. Edward Perera, Daniel Kadin, Ranaweera Bulegoda, Shamalee Damayanthi, Kristina Pringle, Kirula Hettigoda, Jayampathi Palipana, Ayesha Bulegoda, Pasindu Bulegoda, Sean Stroud, and Sunil Shantha also provided invaluable assistance.

Many thanks to my fellow monks and colleagues who have assisted me: Ven. Dr. Pannila Ananda, Ven. Madawala Seelawimala, Ven. Elle Chandawimala, Ven. Pallawela Rahula, Ven. Maitipe Wimalasara, Ven. Shibuya Subhuthi, Ven. Muruthamure Pannaloka, and Ven. Bambarawane Kalyanawansa.

A very special thanks to Cynthia Shimazu (Bodhicari Cintamani) for spending countless hours typing, editing, rewriting, proofing, researching, and generally helping me in every way possible with this book.

Dr. Gamini Jayasinghe has been a true friend, invaluable advisor, and dedicated temple member for more than thirty years. I can't thank him enough for his support.

And finally, many thanks to Shambhala Publications for believing in me and encouraging me to complete this project.

May they all enjoy the blessings of the Triple Gem. May they all be well and happy.

1 ◆ Dealing with Anger

Bee, a frequent visitor to our temple from the Thai community, called me one day asking for an appointment to bring a friend of his for counseling. I asked him what the problem was, and he told me that his friend Tom had asked him to teach him how to use a gun. Bee said that he was surprised at the request, adding that he was very concerned because Tom had also admitted that he had a serious problem with his supervisor at work. Bee said to me, "I will bring Tom to see you; please help him, and teach him how to deal with his anger."

The following day, Bee and Tom visited me in the evening. I took them to the Shrine Hall and chanted a blessing for them. I could tell how uneasy and upset Tom was by the nervous sound of his voice and the angry look in his eye. I asked him whether he wanted to speak to me privately. "No, Bee is my friend, and he knows about my problem. We can discuss it here," Tom said quietly.

"Tom, please tell me why you are so upset. I can see it in every move you make."

"Bhante, for the last two years my supervisor has been harassing me for no good reason. Whatever I do, he criticizes me. When I greet him in the morning, he ignores me. I try my best to please him, but I feel he is always at my throat. I complained to the company's human resources department, and since then his attitude toward me is even worse. He has blocked all chances of my getting promoted, and he makes my life at work a living hell. When I go home, I can't sleep. Even in my dreams I feel like he is torturing me, and sometimes I shout in the middle of the night. My wife wakes me up and tells me I'm grinding my teeth and yelling at someone. I started thinking that the only solution would be to buy a gun, but then I realized that I didn't know how to use one. That's when I asked Bee for help, but Bee told me I had to talk to you first. Bee said you may have another solution. If you do, Bhante, please help me, I'm at the end of my rope."

I listened patiently to Tom's story, and felt sorry for him because I could feel the sad and angry state of his mind. During my years in America I have worked very closely with the Thai community on many occasions, and I was very familiar with their customs and ways of thinking. "Tom," I said calmly, "do you know why the Thai Buddhist flag has a wheel on it?"

"No, Bhante," he replied. He was listening politely to me, with his hands placed together in a sign of respect.

"It is the wheel of Dhamma, representing two important messages. One is the Buddha's first sermon about the Middle Path, which he delivered in Saranath to the Five Ascetics; the second is the Eight Worldly Conditions, which express the duality of our earthly existence. It's this second message that I'd like to explain to you now." I could tell by the look on Tom's face that he was getting impatient with my explanation.

I continued, "Like a pendulum that perpetually swings back and forth, there are four pairs of desirable and undesirable conditions that prevail in this world. Everyone, without exception, must face these pairs of opposites in the course of their lives. What are the four? They are gain (*labha*) and loss (*alaba*); fame (*yasa*) and infamy (*ayasa*); praise (*pasanisa*) and blame (*ninda*); and happiness (*sukha*) and unhappiness (*dukkha*).[1]

"At some point in time, we all have to face unavoidable worldly challenges in each of our lives. But you must remember that although we experience each of these eight conditions, none of them are permanent, and they are continually changing into their opposites, one after the other. It is only by using critical thinking that we can deal with the problems that cause us to suffer—always remembering that they are only temporary, and will soon change."

Tom was looking at me intently, his heart beginning to understand.

"Tom, the Buddha taught us, 'We have to be like the five elements—earth, water, fire, wind, and space. The earth does not get upset by the various things thrown upon it. Nor does water get upset by the various things that it is used to wash. Nor fire, which burns things both clean and dirty without complaint. Nor air, which blows on clean and dirty things equally. Nor space, which is not established anywhere. We need to develop our minds so that like these elements, things that arise that are either agreeable or disagreeable do not invade our minds and remain there. If we conduct ourselves like these five elements, we, too, can remain calm and peaceful, not bothered by whatever happens.'[2]

"This teaching tells us that we must learn that while both agreeable and disagreeable things occur, we are to remain unaffected and undisturbed; if our minds are at peace, we can deal with whatever arises, knowing that the condition will soon change."

Tom replied with frustration. "Bhante, you don't understand. I just want my supervisor to disappear from my life!"

"Tom, did you ever think about what would happen if, in anger, you should harm your boss? You would definitely end up in jail for life. What would happen to your wife and children? Don't you care what happens to them?"

"Of course I do," he replied softly.

"How do you think they would manage without you to support them? Does your wife speak English, and is she working?"

Tom looked down and shook his head from side to side.

"Do you want your family to be put out on the street? Your house and everything you have worked for will be gone because your wife will be forced to pay your legal fees."

Tom seemed to be deep in thought. I recalled a story that I thought might help him, which one of my teachers, Venerable Ananda Maitreya, relayed to me. "Tom, during the First World War, one of the Sri Lankan nationalist leaders was living in Calcutta, India, devoting himself to sharing the Buddha's teachings with others. During this time, Sri Lanka and India were under British rule and a struggle arose in Sri Lanka between the Sinhalese and the Muslims.

"Many Sinhalese leaders in Sri Lanka were arrested and the government imposed martial law. Fearing that the conflict would spread, Sri Lanka's British police inspector general was suspicious of all Sinhalese leaders and he sent messages to his British colleagues in India instructing them to arrest these leaders and return them to Sri Lanka. Although this nationalist leader in Calcutta had nothing to do with the struggle, Calcutta's police inspector general informed him that he was under house arrest and would be deported to Sri Lanka. The inspector general said that he would come to get him in the morning and the man said that he would be ready and would not resist.

"Completely understanding his dire circumstances, the man had a strong feeling that the only way to be saved from deportation was to extend loving-kindness to Calcutta's police inspector general. He placed a photograph of the police inspector general on his desk. He then completely focused his attention on it, extending his feeling of loving-kindness toward the man. In fact, he sat up the entire night looking at the photograph and practicing his loving-kindness meditation.

When the police inspector general arrived in the morning, he approached the man and looked directly into his eyes. He then said, 'I will not send you to Sri Lanka, Sir, but I will instead look after you here as if you were my own father.' Clearly the loving-kindness that was sent to the police inspector general had a miraculous effect—enough to cause him to change the course of his actions.

"Tom, do you think you could try using this practice on your boss instead of inflicting physical harm on him? It might be better than doing something rash and putting your family's survival at risk."

Tom hesitated before answering. "Bhante, I don't think I could even look at my boss's photograph—much less send him good thoughts. What do you expect me to do?"

I could see that Tom was suffering because of his inner turmoil, but he truly did want to find an alternative course of action. "Tom," I said, "loving-kindness is one of the most important meditation practices in our life as Buddhists. Are you willing to learn this?" Tom's eyes were lowered as he nodded yes.

"To practice loving-kindness, or *metta*, you need to find a quiet place where you can release all your tensions and not be disturbed. The place can be a room, a garden—any place that feels comfortable for you. If possible, sit cross-legged, keeping your body erect, and close your eyes. After practicing you will find that you will, as the Buddhist texts say, 'sleep and wake in comfort, see no evil dreams, be dear to humans and nonhumans, and have deities protect you; your mind quickly concentrates, and your countenance is serene.'[3]

"*Metta* should be practiced first toward yourself. If you do not love yourself, can you love others? You can give to others only what you yourself already have; you cannot give what you have not experienced. First, therefore, to practice loving-kindness you have to be friendly toward yourself. Do not burden yourself with an unhealthy guilty conscience. No one is all good, and no one is all bad. Even if you do something wrong, you need not feel guilty. Instead, you should take advantage of the opportunity to correct yourself. You should not mourn over the past, nor brood over the future. Look inside yourself to gently get rid of any feelings of superiority or inferiority that you might have. You will reach a point where unhealthy thoughts and actions will not arise.

"Next, understand that loving yourself means truly appreciating your own value. When you do this, you will also appreciate others and their service to humankind. When you recognize that you are the best you can be at this moment, then you will also realize that others are the best they can be. We can only *be* what we *are*.

"In this way, loving-kindness is also the best antidote for anger. It is the best medicine for those who are angry with themselves, as well as for those who are angry with others. You must learn to extend loving-kindness, *metta*, to all with a free and boundless heart. It has many positive qualities:

Metta is firm, not unstable;
Metta is steady, not shakable;
Metta is gentle, not hard;
Metta is helpful, not interfering;
Metta is dignified, not proud;
Metta is active, not passive;
Hate restricts, but *metta* releases;
Hate brings grief, but *metta* brings peace;
Hate divides, but *metta* unites;
Hate hinders, but *metta* helps;
Metta leads to right understanding;
Metta leads to right thought;
Metta leads to right speech;
Metta leads to right action;
Metta leads to right livelihood;
Metta leads to right effort;
Metta leads to right mindfulness;
Metta leads to right concentration.

"*Metta* teaches us to be hospitable and charitable to one another. It teaches us to speak pleasantly and kindly with one another. *Metta* teaches us to not quarrel among ourselves, but to work for each other's welfare. We even send *metta* to those who hate us, for our enemy in this life may have been our mother, father, brother, or sister in a previous life." Thus, we can reflect:

> This person, when she was my mother in a previous
> birth, carried me in her womb. When I was a baby,
> she cleaned me without disgust. She played with me,
> nourished me, and carried me in her arms. Thus she
> nourished me with deep love. When this person was my
> father in a previous life, he risked his life for me in pursu-
> ing wealth for my comfort. When born as my brother,
> sister, son, or daughter, he or she treated me with loving
> care and gave me every possible help for my welfare. So
> it is unjust for me to harbor anger toward anyone merely
> because of some disagreeable thing done to me in this
> life.[4]

"When anger arises, we can counteract it by remembering the impermanence of all things, both material and mental. The person we might be angry with now isn't the same person he or she was five minutes ago—and neither are we! Understanding that we have both completely changed, mind and body, who or what can I be angry with? Am I angry with hair, nails, teeth, or skin, changeable mental qualities or attitudes?

"By such practice one finds out that one is not angry with an individual person, but with one's own ideas and feelings that are *reflected back* through that individual. This is a good reason to start the practice of extending *metta* toward oneself first." I suggested that he use the following short reflection about *metta:*

May I be free from sorrow and always be happy.

May those who desire my welfare be free from sorrow and always be happy.

May those who are indifferent toward me be free from sorrow and always be happy.

May those who hate me be free from sorrow and always be happy.

May all beings who live in this city be free from sorrow and always be happy.

May all beings who live elsewhere be free from sorrow and always be happy.

May all beings who live anywhere in the world be free from sorrow and always be happy.

May all beings in every galaxy and each element of life in each of those systems be free from sorrow and always be happy.

May we all achieve the highest bliss.

Whatever beings, whether they are timid, strong, tiny or huge, long, average, or short, seen or unseen, living near or far, born or coming to birth, may all these beings have happy and healthy minds.

Let no one deceive another, nor despise anyone anywhere.

Neither in anger nor ill will should one wish harm on another.

As a mother would risk her own life to protect her only child, so should one cultivate a boundless heart toward all.

Let our love pervade the whole world, without any obstructions above, below and across.[5]

When I finished conveying these words about loving-kindness I chanted the Metta Sutta in Pali, knowing that Tom, being Thai, would respond in his heart because he knew I was chanting a blessing for him. Afterward, it was a few moments before Tom could say anything; he was in deep introspection.

Tom finally spoke. "Bhante, your words really calmed me down."

"Good, Tom. You know," I added, "it is not only human beings that can be changed by kind words, but also animals and plants as well. You will be surprised to hear of my own experience when I was a twelve-year-old novice monk." By this time I had Tom's complete attention.

"One day my teacher put me in charge of two jasmine bushes that were growing side by side at the entrance of our temple. Both faced east. The teacher gave equal amounts of fertilizer to each plant. I was requested to give the plants equal amounts of water. Then I was asked to speak kindly to one bush, praising it and admiring it. To the other plant I was asked to use unkind words and belittle it, undermining its importance. I thought it was a really odd—and even a ridiculous—thing to do, but I carried out my teacher's request nonetheless.

"After a few months, to my surprise, I noticed that the plant to which I extended *metta* flourished and bloomed, while the other bush was stunted and did not bear any flowers at all."[6]

Tom gave me a faint smile and said, "I will practice *metta* as you have just taught me, Bhante."

"I hope you will profit from this practice, Tom, and you too, Bee. In this way, according to the Buddha, the suffering will not suffer, the fearful will not fear, and the grieving will not grieve."

Bee and Tom smiled at one another, and I said, "Thank you, Bee, for bringing Tom today. You averted a potential disaster for your friend and his family."

I am happy to report that Tom put into practice the loving-kindness meditation, and his relationship with his supervisor did eventually improve. He is still employed by the same company, and he has been promoted to a supervisor's position himself.

> To become "Noble":
> Do not carry weapons.
> Do not kill.
> Do not cause others to kill.[7]

♦ ♦ ♦ ♦ ♦

2 ◆ Imagination and Reality

One sunny morning I got up earlier than usual and checked my e-mail. To my surprise, there was a message that undermined the reputation of Venerable Truan, a monk who had lived at my temple when he first arrived from Vietnam. Venerable Truan was humble, innocent, energetic, and virtuous. He was excited about his arrival in the United States and was eager to start his own temple.

Within about six months after his arrival he gained enough support from the members of his community to be able to establish his own temple in central California. He appointed me as an advisor, and we kept in close contact. I knew his congregation quite well, since I had participated in many of his religious ceremonies. In fact, I was proud of what he had achieved in the two years since he opened his temple.

The contents of the email, which was from Venerable Truan's board secretary, puzzled me. It said, "Vietnamese monks are vegetarians. Therefore, no fish or meat is brought to the temple. We found chicken fried rice in the refrigerator. In addition, a bottle of wine was on his nightstand. We must remove this type of monk from our temple. There will be a meeting on June 5, 2005, at 3:00 p.m. As advisor, your presence is of utmost importance."

I telephoned Venerable Truan at once, and he immediately came to Los Angeles to see me. "Is there any truth in what your board secretary wrote in the e-mail?" I asked.

"Bhante, it's a complete misunderstanding," he sadly replied. "A group of Thai devotees brought *dana* when they visited my temple for the first time. They were unaware of our vegetarian tradition and brought food that had meat in it. I had my lunch, avoiding the dishes that contained any meat, and went to my room after chanting for the Thai people. Afterward, they had their lunch and then put the leftovers in the refrigerator."

"Honestly, I didn't even notice the food was in there. In the evening Nett, a daily visitor to the temple, saw the leftover food, and without even asking me about it, went home and told his wife about it—and she told everyone else.

"Then, a few days later a bottle of apple cider was presented to me by an American friend. It was the kind with bubbles in it, and the bottle looks just like a wine bottle. After I counseled the American, he left, and I took the bottle to my room. I had a glass before I went to bed, and left the bottle on my bedside table. Duc, who helps me clean up around the temple, saw the cider bottle, and immediately started spreading the rumor that I am an alcoholic.

"You won't believe this. One morning I went to the neighborhood convenience store to purchase a gallon of milk, and that started a rumor that I buy my own liquor, which spread like wildfire. I am fed up with all of this. I just want to disrobe and disappear," he said in utter frustration.

I listened to Venerable Truan patiently and completely understood his unhappy situation; in my many years in the Buddhist clergy I have seen countless examples of such misunderstandings concerning monks by lay people. "Truan, I know you are a virtuous monk," I said. "You have been wrongly accused without the benefit of a hearing. I advise you to please be patient because the truth, like oil, will always rise to the top of the water. As you know, even the Buddha had to face this type of accusation, and he was the Buddha! Perhaps you know the story of Sundari, it is in many of the Buddhist commentaries; I want to tell it as a reminder to both of us because what has happened to you could happen to any good monk.

"Sundari, an unfortunate prostitute, was killed by a group

whose aim was to discredit the Buddha. Her body was hidden in the grove where Buddha and his retinue of monks were staying. When her body was discovered the townspeople accused the Buddha of her murder. They made his stay in their district very uncomfortable.

"Venerable Ananda suggested to the Buddha, 'We should go to another city.'

"'Ananda, if we get the same treatment in the next city, what will we do then?' asked the Buddha.

"'We can move on to another city,' replied Venerable Ananda.

"'Ananda, an elephant trained to fight in a war will never retreat even though arrows come at him from all directions. We monks should be like such an elephant and go forth with our mission, facing criticisms and clearing up misunderstandings.'"

Venerable Truan seemed to relax a bit, having heard this example from the Buddha's time.

Noticing that my talk seemed to comfort him, I continued. "Let me tell you another story about human nature from the time of the Buddha, Venerable Truan.

"One day Atula, a lay disciple who was one of the town leaders, went with his followers to hear Venerable Revata deliver a Dhamma talk. He did not know that Venerable Revata, who was a solitary recluse, would not say anything. After this surprise, Atula then went to Venerable Sariputta, who expounded the Dhamma at great length. Atula found this explanation to be much too long to comprehend. Then he went to Venerable Ananda, who explained the essence of the Dhamma in a nutshell. This time, however, Atula was disappointed because he felt the explanation was too short. Finally, in frustration, Atula went to the Buddha and complained, 'Venerable sir, I went to three monks to try to understand the Dhamma. One was silent, one gave a very lengthy discourse, and the last one said only a few words to explain your teaching. How am I to understand?'

"The Buddha replied, 'There is an ancient saying, Atula: They blame you when you do not talk, they blame you when you talk too much, and they blame you when you talk too little. Whatever you do, they blame you.'"[1]

This seemed to console Venerable Truan. "Furthermore, the Buddha said, 'Just as a solid rock is not shaken by the storm, even so, the wise are not affected by praise or blame.'[2] This reminds me of another story from the Zen tradition that also fits your present predicament.

"There was a Zen master who was virtuous, a highly respected monk. The young, beautiful daughter of a merchant who lived nearby was discovered to be with child, and her parents, understandably upset, tried to find out who the father of the child was. The girl would not say. Finally after much harassment she named the monk.

"The angry parents went to the monk. 'Is that so?' was all he would say. Months later, when the baby was born, the girl's parents took the baby to the monk, handed it to him, and told him to take care of it since he was the father. The monk calmly accepted the baby in his arms, and replied, 'Is that so?' From then on he took on the responsibility of caring for the baby. He had lost his good reputation, but this did not matter to the Zen master.

"A year later the young girl could no longer bear her guilt for lying about the virtuous monk, so she told her parents the truth; the father of the baby was a young man working at the nearby fish market. The parents immediately went to the monk and begged his forgiveness. They asked for the baby, and the monk handed over the baby saying, 'Is that so?'"

Venerable Truan looked noticeably relieved by my stories; he thanked me and left with a light heart.

The date arrived for the special meeting scheduled by Venerable Truan's board of directors. As an advisor I attended, as requested. The meeting started off with a barrage of accusations against

Venerable Truan, who countered by explaining the events as they really happened in an effort to prove his innocence. I noticed, however, that the people did not seem to believe him.

I asked for permission to speak, and took the opportunity to explain the misunderstanding by using a story from the Pancatantra, a collection of Indian fables similar to Aesop's Fables.

"In India, there lived a Brahmin with his wife, and he had a pet mongoose. When the woman gave birth to a son she became wary of the mongoose, fearing that it would harm her baby. The mongoose was in the habit of staying near the baby. The woman, however, always felt that it wasn't safe to leave the infant alone with the animal.

"One day she told her husband to look after the baby so she could go to the market. Upon her return, she saw the mongoose approaching her with a bloody mouth. Shocked, she instantly concluded that the mongoose had killed her baby, and she hit it with her packages, killing it. She screamed and ran into the house. At that very moment her husband appeared, and both parents rushed to the cradle. The baby was in the cradle sleeping, but a huge black snake had been torn to shreds and scattered around the room.

"The woman was heartbroken when she realized she had killed her son's savior. She blamed her husband for being irresponsible and leaving the baby alone.

"Dear members of the board, this story should remind us of the unfortunate outcome that can result from projecting imagined possibilities without any factual basis. It is a fundamental human weakness to enjoy spicy gossip. Unfortunately, some people enjoy spreading gossip, and sometimes they even add made-up details to make it juicier. Little do they realize that they are actually encouraging and harboring unwholesome thoughts that are detrimental to their own spiritual growth. I recollect my mother reprimanding me by saying, 'Son, if you can't say anything nice about someone, then say nothing at all.'

"Socrates, the famous Greek philosopher, had a wonderful test for gossip. One day an acquaintance ran up to him and excitedly said, 'Socrates, do you know what I just heard about one of your students?'

"'Wait a moment,' Socrates replied. 'Before you tell me, I'd like you to take a little test. It's called the Triple Filter Test.'

"'Triple Filter?' asked the man.

"'Yes, that's right,' continued Socrates. 'Before you tell me about my student, let's take a moment to filter what you're going to say. The first filter is Truth. Have you made absolutely sure that what you are about to tell me is true?'

"'No,' said the man, 'actually I just heard about this and—'

"'All right, so you don't really know if it's true,' said Socrates. 'Next, let's try the second filter, the filter of Goodness. Is what you are about to tell me about my student something good?'

"'No, on the contrary—' the man started to say.

"'So, you want to tell me something bad about him, even though you are not certain that it is even true.' The man shrugged, looking down, embarrassed.

"'Well, you may still pass the test,' Socrates said. 'There is still the third filter—the filter of Usefulness. Is what you want to tell me about my student going to be useful to me?'

"'No, not really . . .' mumbled the man.

"'Well, if what you want to tell me is neither *true* nor *good* nor *useful*, why tell it to me at all?' asked Socrates."[3]

Upon hearing this, everyone in the room gave a chuckle, seeing themselves in the story.

I continued, "You can see why people thought so highly of Socrates. We could certainly avoid a lot of problems if we apply this test to anything that we hear before repeating it."

Venerable Truan spoke in front of the others in frustration. "Bhante, these people of my community do not have any *saddha*: they do not have faith in me nor do they appreciate what I do for them. They spend their energy trying to find out about my *sila*, or moral conduct. It is so difficult to work with them," he sighed.

"Yes, Venerable Truan, it is not always easy to work with lay people. Even in the Buddha's time there were incidents where people doubted the sincerity of the monks. It is the habit of some members of the laity to support virtuous monks, as they believe they can seek salvation through the monks' virtues. This has been an age-old practice. Sometimes they have funny ideas about what makes a monk virtuous, like the color of his robe, or what kind of bowl or plate he uses, or other meaningless superficialities.

"If you'll allow me, I would like to relate an interesting story which I believe is relevant to this situation. It was during the Buddha's time, and a devotee wished to offer alms to an *arahat*. He asked the Buddha to find him an *arahat* so he could earn extra merit, and the devotee's wish was instantly fulfilled.

"The *arahat* accompanied the devotee to his house. On the way, there was a small stream and the *arahat* jumped over it without hesitating. This action disappointed the devotee, who believed that an *arahat* should calmly wade across streams and not jump over them. He decided in that moment to give the *arahat* alms only, and not the gift he had planned to give him. When they came to a second stream, the *arahat* slowly waded across in a very dignified manner. The man was confused by the *arahat*'s change in behavior and asked him, 'Venerable sir, at the first stream, you jumped across. Then at the second one you waded across. Why did you change your actions?'

"'My good man,' said the *arahat*, "when I jumped over the first stream you decided not to give me the gift you had planned. If I jumped over the second one, I'd lose my food too.'

"The man gave the *arahat* the intended gift as well as alms, and then went to see the Buddha. 'Lord, please help me to figure out whether I gave alms to a real *arahat* or not. I'm confused. At first the monk jumped over a stream, which I thought was inappropriate. This action caused me to not want to give him the gift I had planned for him, and I decided only to offer him food. The monk must have read my thoughts, so at the next stream he waded across instead of jumping. When I questioned him about the change in the way he was acting, he said that if he had jumped the second time, he wouldn't get his food as well.'

"The Buddha replied, 'There is no doubt, he is a real *arahat*. He jumped across the stream because in his previous life he was a monkey. It was, therefore, an inherent, spontaneous action for a monkey. We all carry our samsaric habits, bringing past-life tendencies into this life—and sometimes even acting like monkeys. We should never judge others simply by their behavior.'"

Venerable Truan interrupted me. "Bhante, I work with many different groups of people, and the others never find fault with me. It is only my own people who always try to find my faults."

I could tell that Venerable Truan was disappointed that his own people were rejecting him. "Venerable Truan, in the Pancatantra, there is an amusing story that goes like this. The leader of the dogs decided to go in search of a new habitat since there was no more food where they were. All the other dogs tried to discourage the leader, but he decided to leave the group anyway. When he departed, his followers advised him to be wary of any wild animals that he might encounter as he traveled. A few days later the leader returned, battered and bruised. All the dogs questioned him in unison. 'Did a coyote attack you? Did a tiger harass you? Or did the jackals bite you?'

"'No, my friends, none of them hurt me.'

"'Then what happened?'

"'I went through the forest, and eventually came to a village. There was a lot of food to eat, and the people were friendly, but I wasn't able to eat anything. My own kind attacked me.'

"'You mean dogs?' they chorused.

"'Yes friends, my own kind. Those dogs did not allow me to eat anything. They attacked me and chased me away.'" At this point, all of the people present at the meeting had a hearty laugh— including Venerable Truan.

"Please, dear people," I said, "I humbly request that all of you support Venerable Truan. I've been acquainted with him since he came to this country, and I know him to be a virtuous monk." I asked that they help him carry out his Buddhist activities and reminded them to always keep in mind the Buddha's words.

I concluded my talk, blessed everyone present, and once again pledged my support to Venerable Truan. I am pleased to say that Venerable Truan is continuing his Buddhist activities in a very efficient manner, and the people of his community no longer gossip about him or each other.

> Showing respect and being humble, content, and grateful,
> Hearing the Dhamma at the proper time;
> This is the greatest happiness.
> Being patient, speaking kind and gentle words,
> Meeting with monks to discuss the Dhamma at the proper
>   time;
> This is the greatest happiness.[5]

◆ ◆ ◆ ◆ ◆

3 • Bamiyan Buddha Statues

It was in March of 2001 that Osama bin Laden, the extremist Islamic fundamentalist, ordered Afghanistan's Taliban leader, Mullah Mohammed Omar, to destroy the famous statues known as the Bamiyan Buddhas, as well as the Buddhist artifacts in the Bamiyan Museum. Bin Laden stated that the statues were "insulting to Islam"—although in fact they were built between the second and fourth centuries c.e., long before Islam even came into existence. These magnificent statues were on the World Heritage Foundation's list of historical sites, and they measured 175 feet and 120 feet high. The taller Buddha statue is believed to have been the world's tallest standing Buddha.

Governments around the world, including neighboring Pakistan, had vehemently protested when they heard about the Taliban's intention to destroy the precious statues. Omar issued a decree calling for the destruction of *all* statues of the Buddha throughout the country, which he declared was in accordance with Islamic law. The Sri Lankan prime minister Ratnasiri Wickramanayake visited Pakistan to work through the Pakistani government, the only open line of communication at that time, to save the statues in an amicable manner. Meanwhile, Sri Lanka's foreign minister at the time, Lakshman Kadiragamar, requested that his envoys in India, Thailand, Myanmar, and Nepal try to work out an international strategy to save the Bamiyan Buddha statues. The Indian prime minister, Atal Bihari Vajpayee, had likewise asked for international help prior to the destruction of these world treasures. He sent letters to the U.S. president, the British prime minister, the U.N. secretary general, and the leaders of several other countries.

Mr. Bihari Vajpayee requested that the Taliban rulers hand over the Buddha statues for preservation. The Indian prime minister said that his government was willing to carefully remove the Buddhas from the location where they had stood for over sixteen hundred years and reassemble them at a new site in India where they could be appreciated by future generations. In the end, however, all discussions and entreaties failed. The Taliban fundamentalists paid no heed to world opinion, and with great arrogance they destroyed the statues with rocket mortars on March 13.

The world's Buddhists grieved in silence over the loss. Hindus, who believe that the Buddha was a reincarnation of Lord Krishna, were outraged at this barbaric, unconscionable act. In fact, Hindu hard-liners in India burned a copy of the Muslim holy book, the Koran, in a public demonstration. The situation became so serious that the Indian government took precautions to prevent a religious uprising against Indian Muslims.

As an attempt to focus world attention on the destruction of the statues, I called upon all Sangha members in Southern California to attend a demonstration that I organized at the 2001 Academy Awards presentation held at the Shrine Auditorium in Los Angeles on March 25. Approximately one hundred Theravada and Mahayana monks and nuns came to hold up banners, one of which said, "Omar, you can destroy Buddha statues, but you cannot destroy Buddha's compassion and love." Our demonstration had its desired effect, and we were seen on television around the world. In addition, several Oscar winners and presenters condemned the destruction of the statues.

After the destruction of the statues various interreligious groups held dialogues in different cities to promote religious harmony. One in Los Angeles was held at California State University, and it was attended by Hindu, Christian, Jewish, Muslim, Sikh, and Buddhist representatives. I was one of the Buddhist representatives. The Hindu delegate was visibly upset by the incident, and he explained the history of Buddhism in India and how it thrived so peacefully alongside Hinduism. Even today the Hindus of India respect the historical Buddha, and they consider Buddhism to be a part of Hinduism. He added that the decline of Buddhism in India was due to the oppressive religious policies of the Moghul invaders whose empire lasted from 1526 to 1707.

I was one of the invited speakers that day, and during my talk I expressed my grief over the destruction of the tallest Buddha statue in the world. I explained that these statues reflected the dominant role played by Buddhism in the region for seven centuries. Bamiyan was a prosperous caravan town on the road to Taxila, the site of a famous Buddhist university in what is now Pakistan, but at that time was part of India. It was this prosperity that made it possible for the construction of the two colossal Buddha statues.

"What has been done by the Taliban, cannot be undone," I said. "We, however, must rise above the ignorant and violent methods of the fundamentalists, and not resort to violence ourselves. The Buddha said, 'Hatred is never overcome by hatred; it is only by love that hatred is overcome. This is an eternal law.'"[1]

I told a story about an incident that happened during World War II in Hiroshima, Japan. "The day the city was destroyed, the renowned sandalwood Buddha statue of one of the outlying temples was completely shattered to bits. When the abbot picked himself up out of the debris and realized he had escaped unhurt and unscathed, he immediately started looking for his monks. His first thought was to send them out into the city to try to help as many people as they could.

"He then noticed a group of monks down on their hands and knees. Some of them were in tears. He went over and asked, 'What are you looking for?'

"A senior monk answered, 'Abbot, we're trying to find as many pieces of the Buddha statue as we can so we can try to glue them back together.'

"The abbot replied, 'Forget the Buddha statue; it's only a piece of wood. Don't even think about trying to repair it. The Buddha is within you—not in the splinters on the floor.'

"One of the monks said, 'Then what should we do, Abbot? Everything is in ruins.'

"'Demonstrate your compassion and love for all living beings and get out there where the people are,' replied the abbot. 'Help the injured and use your common sense. Throw away those pieces of wood and go!'

"The situation we have here is similar. Are we to be motivated by an emotional reaction, or be practical and use our common sense to let everyone know that all Muslims are not violent terrorists? In Afghanistan, Mullah Omar, a supposedly spiritual leader under the influence of bin Laden, performs barbaric acts not only against Buddha statues, but against human beings.

"It is my opinion that ninety percent of the people in Afghanistan are helpless to act, and do not have a voice. The majority are not terrorists. The women cannot work, the girls cannot attend school, and all females are forced to cover their bodies from head to toe and be accompanied by a male escort whenever they leave the home. The most unfortunate fact is that the children don't have enough food to eat and are suffering from malnutrition. At this time, we have to show our compassion for the lives of the innocent children regardless of religious beliefs.

"As Buddhists, we believe in the theory of *kamma* (or *karma* in Sanskrit). There are several classifications or types of *kamma*, which refer to when the effects of kamma are experienced. I feel fairly confident that the terrorists involved in the destruction of the Buddha statues will be punished by an act of nature. The type of kamma that will be operative in this instance is called 'immediately effective kamma,' the kind that takes place almost instantly. The statues were carved in rock, and they represented Gautama Buddha's most dynamic personality. The Bamiyan statues depicted his profound wisdom, great renunciation, his selfless service, and his exemplary, virtuous life. The people of the world venerated the statues for these qualities of greatness. They did not worship them as though they were stone idols. The statues were venerated to demonstrate our gratitude for the Buddha's service to humanity."

As it turned out, within nine months of the destruction of the Buddha statues the United States of America was at war in Afghanistan for other reasons, and the fundamentalist Taliban tyrants who had destroyed the statues were overthrown. This was not exactly the "act of nature" I predicted, but it was definitely a demonstration of "immediately effective kamma."

In early 2002, we held another interfaith conference, just a few months after the terrorist attacks of September 11. We all agreed that the average follower of Islam did not approve of terrorism. It was only a few fundamentalist extremists who had interpreted religious doctrine for their own purposes and created the disaster. We also noted that it is not only Islamic fundamentalists who have been guilty of committing terrorist acts in the past. Throughout history, extremist factions belonging to other religions have wreaked havoc and destruction by twisting their doctrines to suit their political or economic agendas. This has enabled them to recruit followers who are willing to perform terrorist actions on their behalf, motivated completely by blind faith and misinformation.

One Christian representative said that we shouldn't think of taking revenge on terrorists, because it is God's prerogative to punish those who do wrong—not ours. He brought up the example of the destroyed Bamiyan statues in Afghanistan and said that the Buddha had punished those who performed the act.

I became concerned when I heard the man make his comments, and I raised my hand to speak. I said, "I beg your pardon, but you are incorrectly representing the Buddha's teaching. The Buddha was a fully enlightened spiritual teacher who unequivocally practiced compassion and universal love. He also taught us the theory of kamma.

"The Culakammavibhanga Sutta is a short explanation about kamma. Basically it says that all beings are the owners of their actions, the heirs of their actions, and they are bound by their actions; therefore, whatever actions they do, good or bad, they will inherit the consequences.[2]

"According to the Buddha, anyone who acts with anger, hatred, or delusion will not accrue good kamma. Kamma literally means 'action,' and it refers to our intentions with regard to mental, verbal, and bodily behavior. The Buddha's teaching states that every action produces its own specific reaction or effect. So, if one performs wholesome actions, such as donating money to charity, one will experience happiness as the effect or reaction. If, on the contrary, one performs unwholesome actions such as those involving delusion, hatred, or violence, obviously, one will experience suffering as the effect or reaction.

"In Buddhism it is impossible to escape the consequences of one's actions. We are taught that we are the ones who are responsible for our own destinies, and we are not controlled by forces outside ourselves. Our present condition is the result of actions that we have performed in the past. This doesn't mean only our present-day actions; it also means the actions we may have performed in our past lives.

"The effects of our kamma from this lifetime may appear at any moment prior to our death. This type of kamma is called 'immediately effective kamma.'"

I explained that there are actually four classifications of kamma with reference to the time factor involved in reaping consequences.

These are: 1) immediately effective kamma (*dittha-dhamma-vedaniya-kamma*); 2) subsequently effective kamma (*upapajja-vedaniya-kamma*); 3) indefinitely effective kamma (*aparapariya-vedaniya-kamma*); and 4) ineffective kamma (*ahosi-kamma*).[3]

At least one-seventh of all kamma is said to be immediately effective kamma, that which is reaped in the same lifetime. Kamma that cannot be avoided, but is not reaped in *this* lifetime is categorized as subsequently effective kamma, which has its effects in the *next* lifetime. Some actions that are committed do not have their effects in this lifetime or the next lifetime, but in some future lifetime. This is called indefinitely effective kamma. The fourth category, ineffective kamma, arises from spontaneous actions without thought or planning. There is no effect for this kind of kamma. There is also no effect from minor wrongdoing when one's good deeds outweigh the bad. This is another kind of ineffective kamma.

We are the architects of our own fate. What we think, speak, and do comes back to us as our own. It is these thoughts, words, and deeds that are known as kamma. This kamma is like our shadow, and it follows us throughout our lives till the end of samsara.

> Some see what is right as wrong
> And what is wrong as right
> Holding such false views,
> They go to a sorrowful state.
>
> Those who see wrong as wrong
> And right as right
> Hold right views
> And go to a joyful state.[4]

♦ ♦ ♦ ♦ ♦ ♦

4 ◆ Food for Thought

One day when the monks were in the kitchen getting food ready for our midday meal, the front doorbell rang and I went to answer it. Standing before me was a Cambodian lady, around fifty years old, whom I knew I had seen somewhere before, but I couldn't remember where.

I asked, "May I help you?"

"Yes, Lokta," she said, addressing me with the Cambodian word for "teacher." "I have no one else to turn to. My daughter is in the car and she's very sick. She was in the hospital for the last two weeks, but she didn't get better, and the doctors told me to take her home. I decided to bring her here to you first, because she has a ghost living inside of her."

"Please bring her into the temple," I requested.

The woman went to her car, opened the back door, and picked her daughter up in her arms. I thought the daughter was a young child, she looked so small. When she came through the door, however, I saw that she was actually a full-grown woman who probably weighed no more than sixty pounds.

"Please bring her into the shrine room," I instructed the mother, whose name was Nipuni. She carried her daughter and placed her on the floor in front of the Buddha statue. Then she started to cry. There was another woman with the mother, and this friend quickly handed Nipuni a tissue.

I went over to the young woman and sat down on the floor beside her. I tried to talk with her, but she was so weak she couldn't respond. She couldn't even open her eyes.

I asked the mother, "What caused your daughter to be so sick?"

"A ghost," was her reply. "It lives inside her."

"Why do you say that?" I asked.

"Everything she eats, she throws up. She can't take food. Even in the hospital she couldn't eat. They fed her by IV, but after two weeks they said they couldn't do any more. They said there was no reason for her not to eat. Since they could not cure Sarah we knew there must be a ghost inside her. That is why we brought her to see you."

"How long has she been like this?" I asked.

"My daughter used to be bigger than me. She was a normal Cambodian girl—maybe even bigger than normal. The kids in her class at school used to tease her about her weight when she was young, then she started to eat less. Now she won't eat at all. I know it's a hungry ghost inside of her," Nipuni said tearfully.

I immediately called my assistant monk, Bhante Sumanajothi. I told him to go to the kitchen, peel an apple, then mash it into a sauce, and bring it to me.

I gave the mother a cushion to put under the girl's head and then began chanting to her in Pali.

After a few minutes Bhante Sumanajothi returned with the applesauce, and I said to the girl, "If there were any ghosts, they are no longer within you or here at the temple. Buddha's chants have power, and will not allow ghosts to come near you again."

I took a spoonful of the applesauce and put it near the girl's lips. I said, "Please take this apple. It is good for you. There are no ghosts now, and they won't bother you again."

She reluctantly accepted a tiny bit of applesauce, and then another. I slowly kept feeding her until it she had eaten it all. Then I took a length of blessed thread and tied it around her neck as I chanted for her again.

When I realized that she was able to keep the applesauce in her stomach without throwing up, I understood that her disease was mental and not physical. I said to the girl, "You have nothing to fear from eating food. There is no ghost."

The mother had a big smile on her face, and she said, "Lokta, you have made the ghost leave my daughter's body. She will live again because of you."

I explained to the mother, "There was no ghost in your daughter. I believe she has an illness called anorexia, an eating disorder. I imagine long ago when she was in school and was told she was fat, an imprint was left on her mind. Later, she felt she had to starve herself in order to be accepted. That is why she didn't eat. Eventually she couldn't—her body forgot how."

I knew that in Nipuni's home country the belief in ghosts was very strong, so I wasn't surprised at the way she responded.

"The doctor told me the same thing," said Nipuni, "that Sarah had anorexia. But I can't help worrying that she is being harmed by ghosts. I knew you would understand, so I brought her here. I think she was able to eat because no ghost would go near a Buddhist temple, especially in front of a monk like you. When I take her home I'm afraid the ghost will be there and she won't be able to eat again. Will you come to my home and protect our house?" she asked.

"Yes, I will come. Please go home and prepare some soup. I will feed it to her just as I did the applesauce," I replied.

Later that evening I went with Bhante Sumanajothi to Nipuni's house in Long Beach. Sarah was lying in the middle of the living room floor in front of the Buddha statue of their home altar.

I sat down in front of Sarah and said to her mother, "Nipuni, please bring me the soup."

I turned to Sarah, and she said in a weak voice, "Thank you for coming, Bhante."

Bhante Sumanajothi and I chanted in Pali for over an hour. While we were chanting I fed Sarah the chicken soup. She swallowed every spoonful and never indicated her stomach was bothering her.

For three days in a row I went to their house—repeating the same procedure. We chanted while I fed her, and each day she got stronger. After two days she was able to stand up and walk a little bit. After the third day the color had returned to her cheeks and she seemed to be on the road to recovery.

A month later Nipuni called to invite me and my other monks to her house for lunch. When we arrived I couldn't believe my eyes. Sarah opened the door to greet us looking absolutely radiant, healthy, and even younger.

She said, "Thank you so much for coming, Bhante. If it weren't for you I don't think I would be alive today."

In our tradition, after we are given lunch in a devotee's home we give them a Dhamma talk. It wasn't difficult for me to select the topic that day, so I began, "Today we are going to talk about our relationship with food. The word for food in Pali is *ahara*, which means 'that which generates and sustains something.' Without food no one can live in this world.[1] However, when we eat we have to follow the Middle Path, and be careful not to go to any extremes.

"In the Buddha's first sermon he explained the two types of extremes found in human behavior. The first extreme is excess in the pursuit of pleasure and self-gratification; the second extreme is excess in the pursuit of pain and self denial.[2]

"Relating this message to the food we eat, we could say that one extreme is gluttony, or overeating to the point of obesity; the other extreme is anorexia, or starving to the point of death. Sarah, you had anorexia, which is the second extreme. Hopefully, now that you are eating again, you will remain healthy and not go to that extreme again. However, you have to be careful not to have a relapse, which could possibly happen as a result of your thinking that you are overweight and need to diet.

"If you stop eating, Sarah, your family will be very unhappy. They will argue with you, they will argue with each other about how to deal with you, and they will be worried about you—fearing that you might die, like you almost did before your mother brought you to my temple. This will bring you bad kamma, Sarah, so you should consider this as a motivation to keep eating. The Buddha's word for it is *anurakkhana*, which means 'maintenance.' The Buddha strongly encourages us to maintain our bodies and minds so they don't succumb to disease. It is the same with our cars— we have to maintain them or they won't take us where we need to go.

"The opposite of anorexia, Sarah, is the extreme of overeating, or gluttony. The Buddha gave us a wonderful story to illustrate this type of extreme. King Kosala, having just finished a huge meal of rice and curries, approached the Buddha, huffing and puffing. The king paid homage to the Blessed One, and the Buddha realized immediately that the good king had severely overeaten. The Buddha said to him:

Being mindful of how much food one eats,
One avoids discomfort and disease.
With such care,
One goes slowly toward old age.

"The king, upon hearing these words directly from the Buddha, called upon Sudassana, a Brahmin youth in his employ, and said, 'Please learn this verse from the Buddha, and whenever I am taking my meal recite it to me so I should be reminded. I will pay you well for this service.' Sudassana agreed.

"Before too long the king was slim, and very happy with himself. He had gradually reduced his intake of food, thanks to the constant reminder of the Buddha's verse, and he remarked to himself with satisfaction, 'The Blessed One showed compassion toward me in regard to both kinds of good—the good pertaining to the present life and that pertaining to the future life.'[3]

"Let me explain what the king meant by the two kinds of good. When he referred to good in the present life, he was stating how the Buddha's advice on food had made him healthy, energetic, and happy. When he referred to the good in the future life, he was stating how the Buddha's advice on food had prevented him from becoming lazy and slothful, which would have prevented him from meditating and eventually attaining Nibbana," I said, using the Pali term for Nirvana. I went on to explain that the Buddha had this advice about food for monks and nuns, which can apply to everyone:

> With four or five lumps still to eat
> Let one then end by drinking water
> For energetic monks' or nuns' needs
> This should suffice to live in comfort.[4]

"The Buddha knew that staying on the course of moderation, the Middle Path, isn't easy without mindfulness. He reminds us frequently how important it is to examine our thinking, since thinking is what leads us to happiness or suffering, and to help us he gives us pointers from his abundant storehouse of psychological wisdom. In the Majjhima Nikaya he says, 'The characteristics of the mind are thus: if you entertain a desire frequently and dwell upon it, you nourish it and the mind turns toward it, making it grow. Therefore, if there is a thought you want to get rid of, you must avoid giving it nourishment—don't dwell on it, turn away from it, and it will subside.'[5]

"According to Buddhist psychology, our mind is made up of three components: *vinnana*, perception; *mano*, intellect; and *citta*, emotions. Understanding the relationship between these three components is most essential. Each one affects the other, and the relationship between them is in constant flux, from moment to moment. These three define how we see things: what our experiences mean to us, and how we feel about them. They determine how we respond to life as it happens. Ultimately, our response to life initiates our kamma, which influences our rebirth or eventual path to Nibbana."

After we chanted *pirith*—Buddhist suttas chanted for protection—for Nipuni, Sarah, and their family and friends, they all made a promise to come to the temple regularly and try their best to follow the Middle Path. To this day Sarah comes to the temple at least once each month to bring *dana*, and she has remained strong and healthy.

> The wise person considers eating in moderation,
> To put an end to discomfort.
> For the upkeep of the body;
> Not for enhancement,
> Nor for recreation is food eaten.[6]

◆ ◆ ◆ ◆ ◆ ◆

5 ◆ Four Factors for Life

One glorious morning I was deep in thought with a good book when the harsh ring of the telephone interrupted me. It was John, a regular meditator at my temple and a psychologist by profession. He asked to speak with Diana, who he said was meditating in the hall. He also said that the call was urgent. Not only had I never met Diana, I had no idea she was even in the temple.

I immediately walked toward the meditation hall and saw the meditation master who was near the kitchen.

"Sensei, have you seen a woman named Diana?" I asked.

"Yes, she's meditating in the hall, so don't disturb her," he replied.

"John is on the phone for her and he says it's urgent," I answered, continuing toward the hall.

To my amazement, when I opened the door, I heard loud crying and sighing. I saw a tall Caucasian woman who seemed to be in her late twenties, leaning against the opposite wall, crying her heart out. I hesitated for a moment, then walked over and handed her the phone, saying there was a call from John. She took the phone from me without saying a word, so I left and returned to my office.

Ten minutes later she found her way to my office and returned the phone.

"Please sit down," I said to her, because she looked upset.

"Thank you," she replied. "My name is Diana, but I don't know what to call you."

"You can call me 'Bhante,' which means 'spiritual friend.' What brings you to our temple today?"

"My therapist, John, told me to come here to meditate. He brought me here the first time and introduced me to Sensei," she answered.

Diana seemed to be under a great deal of stress. I asked her to follow me into the shrine room and tried to make her feel comfortable.

"What is bothering you, Diana?" I asked.

"I can't sleep, Bhante. There are ghosts in my apartment," she replied with fear in her voice.

"Please relax for a while, Diana, and I will chant for you to remove the ghosts."

I chanted for her in the Pali language, which is the actual language the Buddha spoke. Since the Buddha's time, Pali has never changed; it is no longer a spoken language, but like Latin it is used for religious texts. The Pali chants carry with them a special vibration that can actually change spatial energy and inject a positive influence on those who hear them. The chants are usually suttas, or sermons given by the Buddha himself. They express the Buddhist philosophy, and they transmit the Buddha's teaching from generation to generation. Ever since the suttas were first uttered by the Buddha, there has never been a time on the planet when they were not being chanted, somewhere—by Buddhist monks who continue to carry on this ancient oral tradition.

The power in the Pali chants transcends logical explanation. The Buddha originally taught the Ratana Sutta in Visala City, India, because the city had a problem with ghosts, disease, and hunger. The Buddha's disciple, Venerable Ananda, chanted this sutta while walking through the city sprinkling holy water. It wasn't long before the city returned to normal. This is the sutta that I chanted for Diana that morning.[1]

After I finished chanting I said, "I'm going to tie this holy thread on your wrist to remind you that you are now free from the ghosts that may have been bothering you, and to help you get a good night's sleep." When I was done, she looked up at me and I sensed that she was somewhat relieved.

However, early in the evening, much to my surprise, she came back to the temple with a pillow under her arm, telling the monk who opened the door that she came to sleep over. The monk asked her to wait while he went to get me.

"Bhante, can I sleep here tonight? There are ghosts in my apartment."

"Diana, there are no ghosts in your home. We took care of that earlier today with the chanting. Please go home—you cannot stay here. This is a monastery for monks only, and women are not allowed to sleep here. You are welcome to come for our scheduled meditation sessions, but you must return home afterward."

"How can you chant here and expect the ghosts in my apartment to go away," she argued. "You didn't chant in my apartment!"

"Diana, you have the blessed string on your wrist, and I'll give you some holy water to sprinkle throughout your apartment. I assure you that you have nothing to fear."

She didn't say a word, and reluctantly turned away and left the temple.

The following day during meditation class in our old hall, I heard deep breathing coming from the individual meditation room. I looked around the room and noticed that the others were hearing it as well. One meditator was disturbed by the sound, so he spoke up and asked me what it was. I told him that it was nothing to worry about, and we resumed our session. I had a strong feeling that it was Diana.

Usually we conclude our session with the loving-kindness meditation. Sending out our positive energies to everyone we know, as well as everyone in the universe, is a very special moment for all of us. I asked one of the meditators, a doctor named Victor Coronado, to bring the person out of the little room so she could join us. He opened the door and then very quickly shut it, saying we shouldn't bother the woman. He didn't want to disturb the rest of the group in our closing moments.

After the meditation I walked over to the door to find out what was going on. Before I could open it, the doctor jumped up and put his hand on the door, preventing me from opening it. "Don't open it, Bhante! There's a naked woman in there," he said.

I turned to one of our female meditators, Khema (Carol Munday Lawrence), and asked her to get the woman dressed.

It took over an hour for Khema to convince Diana to put her clothes on, but she finally did. The two women came to the shrine room, and Khema took me aside to tell me what a struggle it had been to convince Diana to get dressed. Diana had argued with her, saying, "I trust the monks, and they should trust me too—so bodily coverings aren't necessary." Khema explained to her that the monks practice celibacy, and they should not be distracted.

I went to the shrine room with Khema to talk to Diana. I questioned her about her personal life, in an attempt to understand her strange behavior. She confided in me that she was employed at an insurance company, and that a coworker had gotten her to attend a three-day seminar for which she had paid eight hundred dollars.

The seminar was about relationships—about overcoming the fears and obstacles that stand in the way of forming them. Diana told me she had never had a relationship with a man, and that she was frustrated. The speaker at the seminar had focused on human behavior and how one's apparel influences it. According to him, all the problems in society arose as a result of the clothes people wore. He said that when a person's body is covered up with clothing, curiosity arises. He used the illustration that animals have no problems because they are naked. Furthermore, he said that human suffering is completely due to our wearing clothing.

I silently felt sympathy for Diana's naive nature, felt sorry for how gullible she was.

"Diana, do you know the difference between humans and animals?" I asked her.

She looked at me, not comprehending.

I continued, "According to the Pali and Sanskrit languages, *manussa* or *manusha* means 'developed mind'—which describes a human being. *Tiracchana* means animal, or one whose mind is not developed. We human beings have a code of ethics, whereas animals do not. Humans and animals both need to sustain themselves to stay alive—however, there is a difference in their modes of existence. Both humans and animals need food, water, air, and sleep. Humans can experience embarrassment, but animals cannot.

"According to the Buddha there are two primary psychological factors that influence human behavior in such a way that it prevents them from committing wrong acts. In Pali they are called *hiri*—that is, self-respect—and *ottappa*—or self-preservation. These factors contribute to the overall level of decency and orderliness of society.

"The Buddha emphasizes the importance of these psychological factors by saying that if not for them, there would be no consideration for one's reputation or family and societal relations. He says that without them people would live like ordinary animals. Self-respect keeps us on a positive, pure, and maturing path that is part of living a rich and full life, while self-preservation protects us from succumbing to the temptation to commit wrongful acts. They work together in our minds and serve as protective shields against our thinking, saying, or doing negative and unwholesome thoughts, words, or deeds."

I continued by explaining the four factors of *iddhipada*,[2] the way to have a successful and peaceful life.

"I'd really like to hear those, Bhante," Diana said.

"These four factors, according to the Buddha, are *chanda, viriya, citta,* and *vimamsana.*[3] The first one, *chanda,* means aspiration," I began. "It is that which we hope to achieve, a worthy goal that we are lovingly dedicated to attaining. Let me illustrate *chanda* using an ancient Sri Lankan legend.

"Long ago there was a king who was very fond of sweets, and every week there would be a particular cake that he enjoyed above all others because it tasted sweeter than anything he had ever eaten. He became curious to find out how it was prepared.

"He sent out special members of his court to find out the secret of the delicious cake, and they all returned with different odd stories. All these different stories baffled the king because they really made no sense. He was so determined that he decided to disguise himself as a laborer to discover the secret. To his surprise he found that all the reports he had been given by his courtiers were completely untrue. In actuality, the king found the cook of the special cake to be a blind man who was very poor. The man lived in a small shack.

"The king spoke kindly to the poor man and befriended him. He offered to help him prepare his cake. The blind man was very happy to have the help of a new friend.

"While they were preparing the cake the man offered the king a small sample to taste. Once again the king was amazed at the wonderful, sweet flavor—the most excellent cake he had ever tasted. 'What ingredients do you use in your cake, my friend? It is absolutely delicious.'

"The poor man replied, 'Friend, I use the same ingredients as everyone else does.'

"'Then why is it so sweet? To me it is different from all others,' replied the king.

"'What makes my cake sweet, my friend, is my desire to produce the very best cake I can. This desire comes from deep within me. Our king is a kind, compassionate, virtuous, and righteous ruler. I make this to show him my appreciation and gratitude.'

"'Is that so?' the king replied, astonished.

"'Yes, my friend. It's just the same as a mother cooking for her child. The only difference in the ingredients she uses and those that others use is her love. It is the same with me. I enjoy cooking for my king, and the whole time I am stirring the ingredients I am repeating to myself over and over, "May he be well, happy, peaceful, and prosperous." I am always sending him *metta*,' was the blind cook's reply.

"The king was overwhelmed by the man's kind words, and he remained speechless for a few moments.

"The blind man finally asked, 'Are you still here?'

"The king cleared his throat and said, 'Yes, my dear friend, I am still here. But I am not who you think I am. I am your king. I came to find out what made your cakes so much sweeter and more delicious than the rest. You have given me an answer that is more precious to me than gold. You, my friend, remind me of my father, and I will take care of you as if you were he. Come with me to the palace so we can enjoy each other's company. You have taught me the true meaning of the sweetness of right action.'

"The cake maker proved that whatever one does, if it is performed with a heart filled with loving-kindness, the outcome will be nothing less than excellent. Therefore, one must demonstrate a burning desire to bring about the best results when performing any action, no matter how small or humble."

Diana spoke up and said, "Unfortunately, now that the poor cake maker is in the palace, the king will miss out on his special sweets," a remark that made us all laugh.

I continued, "Now back to our four factors. The second factor for achieving one's goal is *viriya*, which means 'concentrated effort.' A strong, determined, concentrated effort must be exerted when one performs any action. *Viriya* is the same kind of effort that the Buddha demonstrated when he sat down under the Bodhi Tree and said, 'Let skin and sinews and bones waste away, let flesh and blood in my body dry up; yet there shall be no ceasing of energy until I attain enlightenment.'[4]

"The third factor is *citta*, which here means visualizing one's goal. *Citta* as the emotional aspect of mind is used here. The mind is not a separate entity, distinct from emotions. For example, if one's goal is to become a medical doctor, and the individual puts posters saying 'Doctor' all over his room, then he is reminded of his goal all the time. This will help him to focus the energy to achieve it.

"The fourth factor is *vimamsana*, which means 'resourcefulness.' When one does not succeed in one's first attempt to achieve a goal, one must look into other avenues or methods for achieving it without giving up. A shining example is the life of Siddhartha Gotama. Upon leaving his father's palace, he went first to the ascetic Alara Kalama for instruction. After learning everything that this teacher knew, Siddhartha's goal of enlightenment was still not achieved, so he decided to leave and seek another. Next he went to Uddaka Rama. With this teacher the result was the same. Siddhartha then decided to starve and torture his body, engaging in the then-common practice of self mortification for spiritual achievement. He found that this only made him weak, physically and mentally. Finally, he decided that this method was not helping him and he made up his mind to follow a Middle Path, which led him to full enlightenment, his desired goal. We can see from this example that the Buddha never gave up—and he was never afraid to change his course and try something new to achieve his goal.

"Now, the two of you have heard of four factors for a successful life, and I am confident that if you follow them and practice them with *viriya*, then you will be able to accomplish your goals in life.

At the same time you will earn the blessing of being able to help others. And, Diana, no more seminars for you—just use these four factors for life."

They thanked me profusely, and Diana left the temple. I extended my gratitude to Khema, who had handled Diana so skill-fully earlier in the evening. To my surprise, one day I received a letter from Diana along with a donation. She was in Iowa, leading a contented life guided by the Buddha's teachings.

> Do not believe in anything
>> simply because you have heard it.
> Do not believe in traditions because
>> they have been handed down for many generations.
> Do not believe in anything because
>> it is spoken and rumored by many.
> Do not believe in anything simply because
>> it is found written in your religious books.
> Do not believe in anything merely
>> on the authority of your teachers and elders.
> But after observation and analysis,
>> when you find that anything agrees with reason and
>> is conducive to the good and benefit of one and all
> Then accept it and live up to it.[5]

◆ ◆ ◆ ◆ ◆ ◆

6 ◆ Are Buddhists Idol Worshippers?

Anup and his family, Buddhists who were originally from Calcutta, India, visited me at my *vihara* (temple) in Los Angeles shortly after they immigrated to the United States. I first met them when I was studying at Calcutta University in the early 1970s. They settled in Los Angeles because they felt it was the best place to educate their daughter, the weather was agreeable, and there were Buddhist temples in the area where they could have spiritual fellowship. Anup appeared to be very ambitious and often spoke of getting rich quickly. At the time of his first visit to my temple he was employed as a landscaper. He was a very respectable man; he was a teetotaler and was very family oriented. His one indulgence, however, was an occasional foray into the world of gambling, because he firmly believed he would one day hit the jackpot. Since he was a temperate man, he never became addicted to gambling, and it never affected the well-being of his family.

One day I said to him, "Anup, you are such a good man, why do you insist on gambling?"

He replied, "Bhante, you know that I would never do anything to hurt my family. I only gamble from time to time because I want them to have the best life possible here in America. Besides, I truly believe that one day I'll get rich. It is my fondest dream."

"You may or may not get rich here in America, Anup. Only time and your own hard work might accomplish that. In the meantime, you must set a good example for your children in regard to earning money, because if you get easy money they may learn the wrong lesson. America, you must remember, can become a very disappointing—and even a tragic—place for newcomers who are only interested in getting rich quick. You must be very careful, Anup, to build the proper foundation for your financial well-being."

"I understand, Bhante, but if we have money we can be happy. If I have money I can even help you build a new temple here in Los Angeles," he replied.

His statement caused me to think that Anup needed to be reminded of the Buddha's words about how contentment brings happiness.

"Anup, the Buddha preached that we must find contentment within ourselves and not spend our lives only chasing money. He said, 'Happiness follows the one who thinks, speaks, and acts with a pure mind.'[1] It is a fact that money is essential to live, but we should learn not to be a slave to money."

"Bhante, you know that I work as a landscaper, and most of our customers are in Beverly Hills. You should see how the people live there—huge houses, expensive cars, swimming pools, and tennis courts. I see the people going in and out of their houses sometimes and they look really happy. It's all because of their money, and that's why I want it so badly."

"But Anup," I replied, "You're only looking from the outside. You can't really see what's going on with those people on the inside of their rich homes. A member of my temple who lives in Beverly Hills arranged for me to teach meditation classes in the homes of some of her friends. Every week we rotate and visit a different home in Beverly Hills, where we meditate and I give a Dhamma talk. One day, in one of those huge, rich homes, I went to the bathroom and, out of curiosity, I opened the medicine cabinet. I know I shouldn't have done this, but I had never been in a home like that before. Anyway, the medicine cabinet was full of prescription medicine for sleeping and relaxation. I was shocked. I, too, thought that the rich people who lived like this would be happy and not need medicine to sleep or relax. Anup, these people are not happy because of their money."

Anup gave me a look that told me he was still not convinced.

"Anup, I remember being told a fairy tale in school when I was a child, about King Midas. Have you ever heard it?"

"I'm not sure, Bhante, although the name seems familiar."

"King Midas was very, very rich and had a great room full of gold. He liked gold so much he even named his only child 'Marigold.' Every day he would sit in his room, counting his golden money, thinking that gold was the best and most wonderful thing in the world. One day a fairy appeared before him and asked, 'King Midas, if I should grant you one wish, what would you ask for?' King Midas said, 'I would ask that everything I touch should turn to beautiful yellow gold.'

"The fairy told him that at sunrise the next day his wish would be granted. And he was warned that it would not make him happy. The next morning the king woke and waited for the sunrise. Just as the fairy said, at sunrise the chair he was sitting in turned to gold. The king was wild with joy. He ran around the room touching everything and watching it turn instantly to gold. Of course he became hungry, but when he tried to eat, the food turned to gold. He tried to drink a glass of water, but it also turned to gold.

"Then his daughter, Marigold, came running in from the garden and hugged him. Instantly she turned into a golden statue. He was struck with grief and fear and cried out to the fairy who had given him the gift. He offered everything he had if only his little daughter would be restored. The fairy appeared and asked him if he still thought gold was the best thing in the world. The king said that he had learned his lesson and that he no longer thought gold was everything. Of course in a fairy tale everything can change back to normal, but sometimes in real life it is not so easy to fix our mistakes.

"The Buddha said, 'When you catch a serpent you have to grab it by the head and not the tail, because if you grab it by the tail it can coil around your arm and strike you.'[2] It is the same with money. If a person obtains money in a way that is questionable, or illegal, or through greed, it is the same as grabbing a poisonous serpent by the tail. It will eventually turn and destroy the person who obtains it.

"So, Anup, the way one obtains money is of utmost importance. Quickly winning the jackpot might one day lead to your downfall. You must learn to earn and use money wisely; otherwise you and your family may wind up suffering."

Anup thanked me for the lessons, but I could tell that he still wasn't convinced. However, his wife, Purnima, and their daughter, Deepa, seemed very grateful that I had taken the time to explain about money. Purnima said, "I have been telling Anup similar stories for years, but he never listens to me. Perhaps yours and the Buddha's stories will help him learn and change his mind. The truth is, we always seem to have enough money and we are happy with our lives."

Anup had a good friend named Neal, who was also from a Buddhist family in Calcutta. Neal, however, converted, and joined a fundamentalist Christian group upon his arrival as an immigrant in America. This group convinced Neal that Buddhists were idol worshipers and that Buddhist temples were the homes of the "devil." Neal and Anup carpooled to work and from time to time Anup would stop by my temple on his way home. Neal would refuse to come inside, choosing to wait for him in the parking lot. A couple of times I went out to the car to speak with Neal, but he would only look away and would not even speak to me.

Neal did his best to convince Anup to join his Christian group, and after continual repeated attempts he finally succeeded. Eventually, Neal also convinced Anup to remove the Buddha statue from his home—telling him that it was an idol, and that to have it there was idol worship. Neal was very clever and knew exactly what motivated Anup—money. Neal finally convinced him by saying that he could never achieve material success if he had an "evil" Buddha statue in his home; he must get rid of it if he was to succeed.

Meanwhile, Purnima and Deepa had refused to have any part of Anup's new faith, and they rebuffed any attempts he and Neal made to convert them. They were both determined to remain Buddhists. Neal's constant proselytizing became so aggressive and offensive that the mother and her teenage daughter had finally forbidden him to come to their house. This caused a deep rift between Anup and the rest of the family. The mother and daughter understood Anup's obsession with money, and they could see the connection it had to his new faith. They knew that Anup sincerely believed what Neal and his newfound friends told him, that he would get rich if he followed the fundamentalists' belief and no longer worshipped evil idols.

The Buddha statue had been presented by me to Anup and his family as an arrival gift when they came to this country. The statue was revered and dearly respected by Purnima and Deepa, and I learned later that they were horrified to come home one day and find that it had disappeared.

Anup came home from work that evening and thirteen-year-old Deepa had run to him and cried out that the Buddha statue was gone. "Do you know what happened to it, Daddy?" she asked in tears.

"The Buddha statue wasn't making us rich. So why should we keep it?" he asked.

"Daddy, you had no right to get rid of our statue. It belonged to the family. Bhante Piyananda gave it to us when we came to America! How could you?" she cried.

"That statue is an idol and it doesn't belong in our home. I had to take it away or we would never get rich," Anup replied.

Purnima entered the room and said, "Money has become your idol, Anup, and Neal has brainwashed you with these silly ideas. The Buddha statue has nothing to do with idolatry. It is a symbol of compassion and love—feelings you know nothing about. You only care about money. Shame on you!"

Deepa continued, "Your karma will be cursed because of what you've done, Daddy. You have no idea what this will do, not only to you, but to all of us." This last remark hit home, and frightened Anup.

After this exchange Purnima and Deepa had grabbed a few personal items and put them in a suitcase. They left the house without saying another word to Anup. Later in the evening Anup found out that they had gone to stay with a cousin.

The following day, Anup fell off a ladder while he was working and injured his back. He was hospitalized for three days and in bed for another week. As soon as Purnima and Deepa heard about Anup's accident they rushed back home to care for him.

When he was brought home from the hospital Purnima called me to tell me that Anup had been hurt. I immediately paid a visit to Anup's bedside with a senior monk, and I asked Purnima to bring the Buddha statue so we could do *pirith*, chanting a Buddhist sutta for protection.

The custom is to place a small bowl of water in front of the Buddha statue, put the end of the *pirith* string in the water, wind the string around the Buddha statue, have the monks hold the string, and give the other end of the string to the patient to hold. While the patient is holding the string we chant for him. When we finish we tie a piece of the string around the patient's wrist with a blessing of protection and recovery. Afterward, we give the water from the bowl to the patient to drink for good health.

Purnima left the room, and I assumed she was going to get the Buddha statue. Deepa came into the room shortly afterward and took the chain from around her neck, from which was suspended a tiny Buddha. She said, "Here, Bhante, you can use this Buddha for the ceremony." I was surprised and puzzled that they hadn't brought their Buddha statue to me, but I didn't ask any questions. I used her tiny Buddha for the ceremony, and ultimately gave Anup the water to drink. I also applied the special herbal oil, which we had brought from the temple, to his back.

While we were still there, his pain suddenly eased. He got out of bed, took a few steps, and thanked us with both hands held together.

After a few weeks, Anup came to the temple with his wife and daughter. He quickly explained the purpose of his visit: he wanted to ask me for a Buddha statue.

I was surprised at the request. "Why do you want another Buddha statue?" I asked. "I gave you one not so long ago when you arrived here in America."

Anup replied, "Bhante, I did a foolish thing and made a horrible mistake."

Before he could complete his sentence, Purnima spoke up and said, "Bhante, he got rid of the Buddha statue when he joined Neal and became a fundamentalist Christian. Neal even told him that it was the devil."

Anup then said, "No more, Purnima. I have given it up. I have been punished. I know it wasn't from the Buddha, but since I converted my life has been in turmoil. Then I had my accident. I don't want to be a part of that group any more."

Before I could respond, Deepa said, "Bhante, may I ask you a question?"

"Yes, Deepa, what is it?"

"Daddy's friend Neal, the man who made him go to that church, called us idol worshippers for having the Buddha statue in our house. Is this true? Are we idol worshippers?"

"Deepa, do you worship the Buddha—or do you worship a lifeless statue?"

"Bhante, when I see the serene face of the Buddha statue I feel calm and peaceful. I see it and I remember the stories of the Buddha's compassion and wisdom. I think about the Buddha, his character and teachings—not the statue," the wise young girl replied.

"You are absolutely correct, Deepa. If we really look closely at the face of the Buddha statue, we can see in it the embodiment of compassion and love, as well as its character and the strength of its teaching. We in turn enjoy—if only for a moment—a sense of boundless joy. Therefore, I firmly believe that by venerating the Buddha we can experience a sense of his superior qualities. Even if we visualize the Buddha, this can help us gain inner calmness and a serene outlook."

Purnima then asked, "Bhante, tell us how we should venerate the Buddha?"

"We should venerate the Buddha as part of our daily practice," I said, "and every time we practice we should recall his firm determination to attain enlightenment. He said, 'Though my skin, my nerves, and my bones shall waste away and my lifeblood dry up, I will not leave this seat until I have attained Supreme Enlightenment.'[3] He did not cease until that is attained which can be won by human strength, human energy, and human effort.

"This teaches us that we have to strive hard to achieve our goals. The Buddha attained enlightenment under the Bodhi Tree that gave him shelter in Buddha Gaya. He immediately showed his gratitude to the tree by keeping his eyes on it for seven days. From this we should learn about the need to show our gratitude to those who help us."

Anup said, "I would like to show my gratitude to my wife and daughter for their patience with me during the time I was worshipping the idol of money." He then turned to his wife and said, "Purnima, do you want me to look at you for seven days to show you my gratitude?"

Purnima laughed and said, "I don't need you to do that to show your gratitude to me, but I do need you to look at things clearly and not be deceived by people who might lead you away from what you know to be true."

Then Deepa added, "Where is the Buddha you got rid of—the one Bhante Piyananda gave us? That is our family Buddha statue. Can you please bring it back?"

Anup suddenly became downcast upon hearing this request. After a moment he said, "Deepa, I wish I could, but I can't. Neal took that statue and had it destroyed. Let's just look at this as another good lesson about the impermanence of all things, okay? Please forgive me."

I excused myself for a moment and went to my room. I returned with a beautiful seated Buddha statue and handed it to Deepa.

"This is your new family Buddha, Deepa. I'm sure your father will show more respect to this one."

Anup, Purnima, and Deepa bowed to me with gratitude and thanks.

I said, "Deepa, why do we offer to the Buddha statue incense, flowers, and candles? Traditionally, every Buddhist in the world performs this ritual."

"I'm not really sure, Bhante, except I know that I feel good when I do it," she replied.

"The Buddha was a living embodiment of all of the greatest virtues, which fall into three main categories: highest morality (*sila*), deepest concentration (*samadhi*), and most penetrative wisdom (*panna*). These qualities of the Buddha were unsurpassed and unparalleled in human history.

"When we offer incense, we are recalling the great virtues of the Buddha. We are determined to cultivate these virtues within ourselves.

"The offering of flowers, which we arrange in an appealing manner, will cause the individual to think of organizing his or her life in an orderly and appealing manner. Flower offerings also help us to understand impermanence as part of life, as exemplified by the fading away of these flowers. We begin to realize that life itself is similar to the flowers, and that we ourselves will one day pass away.

"The lighting of candles, and offering light, is a reminder that we continually need to bring illumination and clarity to our lives. Since the Buddha represents the highest wisdom, the lighting of the candles symbolizes the shining of light where once there was darkness. The Buddha said that wisdom could be achieved in three ways: listening and studying, experimenting and analyzing, and meditating, the gateway that leads us beyond to wisdom.[4]

"Deepa, when we pay homage to the Buddha we say a chant beginning with *"Itipi so bhagava, araham, samma . . . ,"* I began, but then I realized it might be more useful to offer her the following translation:

Such indeed is the Blessed One,
Perfected, fully awakened,
Endowed with knowledge and virtue,
Having walked the right path,
The knower of worlds,
Incomparable guide of willing persons;
Teacher of gods and humans; awakened and blessed.[5]

"I'd like to tell you all a story about the late first prime minister of India, Sri Jawaharlal Nehru," I continued, "and the great results he achieved by venerating the Buddha. Would you like to hear this story?"

"Yes, Bhante, please," replied Deepa, Purnima, and Anup in unison.

"Nehru had been jailed by the British for being a freedom fighter. In his jail cell in Dehra Dun in northern India he was very depressed because of the bad treatment and the poor living conditions he encountered there. It was during this period that he received a picture of the Buddha from his friend Bernard Aluvihara of Sri Lanka. The picture was of the Samadhi Buddha statue in Anuradhapura. He placed the picture in his cell, and he began to treat it as his companion. He recounted that very soon he began to receive positive energy from contemplating the photograph, as he reflected upon the willpower of the Buddha.

"While looking at the Buddha he questioned himself, 'If a sculptor, without seeing the Buddha, could carve a statue representing the wholesome qualities of the Buddha, I should also be able to develop the willpower of the Buddha by visual veneration, and thereby be able to free my people and my land from colonial rule.'[6]

"When he became the first prime minister of independent India, he went to Sri Lanka to pay homage to the Samadhi Buddha statue."

Purnima turned to her husband and said, "Nehruji was surely not worshipping an idol when he paid his respects to that Buddha statue, Anup. He was expressing his gratitude for the inspiration he received from the Buddha, which enabled him to free our country."

Anup and his family continue to live happy Buddhist lives in Los Angeles. Anup has given up his "get rich quick" ideas and found contentment.

It is good to see the Noble Ones;
And blissful to live among the wise.

Not encountering fools, one will have happiness.
The company of the foolish brings pain.
It is like being partners with an enemy.

The company of the wise brings happiness.
It is like being with one's beloved family.

Follow the Noble One,
He who is steadfast, wise, learned, dutiful, devoted,
Truly good and discerning,
Follow as the moon follows the path of the stars.[7]

♦ ♦ ♦ ♦ ♦ ♦

7 ◆ A Catastrophe

On December 26, 2004, a horrific earthquake occurred near Indonesia, which resulted in a tsunami that devastated the surrounding countries. Sri Lanka and Indonesia were the hardest hit.

The moment the news reached us here at our temple in Los Angeles, we were inundated with telephone calls offering help. I could tell many stories about the kindness we were shown by both friends and complete strangers. Some friends in Hollywood set up an organization to collect funds from members of the entertainment industry. A prisoner in Texas sent us fifteen dollars. Children in several private schools pooled their piggy banks and collected money for us. Of course our temple members worked very hard collecting many thousands of dollars, especially the Sri Lankan children. We set up a committee and started collecting funds for rehabilitation and rebuilding in Sri Lanka. We are happy to say that we completed the goal of our housing project. We built and presented thirty-seven houses to tsunami survivors in the Galle district.

It brings me sadness to state here that the personal opinions of some of the world's religious leaders and scholars were less than compassionate. Some believed that the tsunami was a punishment from God because the people did not follow his commandments. Others suggested that the tsunami disaster was due to bad kamma as a result of the victims' livelihood, or perhaps it was due to bad collective kamma from their previous lives.

We had to face and overcome many obstacles in our efforts to collect funds for the victims. For instance, one ethnic group leader named Pon tried to discourage me by saying, "Do not accumulate bad karma by helping the fishermen."

"Why do you say that?" I asked.

"In Buddhism, the First Precept forbids the killing of any living thing. These people have lived a life against this Buddhist principle, so they got what they deserved," he said.

I was shocked by his narrow-mindedness. "Pon, these people have lost everything," I replied. "This is the time to show our compassion regardless of their livelihood. Compassion means feeling another's pain. It means sensitively being aware of another person's situation and feelings. It means listening with your whole being and giving, if you can, what is relevant and appropriate. Compassion is spacious and very generous. Compassion is environmental generosity, without direction. It is filled with spontaneous joy in the sense of trust. Generosity is an important component of compassion, which arises from the deepest recesses of your heart. And perhaps most importantly, compassion does not coexist with judgments."

Pon asked, "Bhante, don't you believe in Heaven and Hell?"

"I believe that Heaven and Hell are both here now, Pon. If you perform an action and derive happiness by seeing another person's joy, then you are in Heaven. If by your action you are unhappy or you make another person unhappy, then you are in Hell. We derive happiness when we share."

"As a Buddhist monk, you are supposed to believe in Heaven and Hell. I'm surprised you gave me the new interpretation you just did," Pon said self-righteously.

"I would like you to hear this folk story told in India and China," I replied. "One day an ascetic who was renowned for his power to do miracles was questioned by a pupil, who challenged: 'Sir, you claim to be able to perform miracles. Could you show me Heaven and Hell?'

"The ascetic looked at him silently for a while. In a few

moments, lo and behold, right there in front of them appeared a large table filled with a sumptuous banquet. A group of people with sad, mournful faces appeared around the table. They couldn't bend their arms at the elbows, so they couldn't eat. They tried to eat but failed time and again. They became frustrated and angry. Even though they were starving they scattered food everywhere, making a complete mess, and they left hungry. 'That is Hell,' the teacher said to the student as the scene faded.

"'Please show me Heaven,' said the student. The ascetic nodded, and in a few moments there appeared a similar table laden with great heaps of delicious-looking food. A group of smiling people walked in and stood around the table. These people also could not bend their arms at the elbows. With very little deliberation they figured out how to put food on their spoons and reach across the table to feed the person on the other side. In this manner, they were able to feed each other, and they all enjoyed the banquet and went away happy and satisfied.

"The teacher smiled and said, 'That is Heaven!'

"The student understood from this lesson that sharing with others brings satisfaction and happiness. He also understood from the first scene, depicting Hell, that selfishness, and thinking only of oneself, can lead to separation, unhappiness, and misery.

"Furthermore, the ascetic explained to him, 'Compassion is the complete reflection of overall harmony. It contains the essential ingredients of care, responsibility, respect, and knowledge. It is vital to feel caring for others and to feel concern for what may happen to them.'"

I could see that Pon was still not totally satisfied with my explanation. I continued, "The Buddha gave a talk about the five laws governing the order of things, or *niyama*.[1] The first law, Pon, is *utu niyama*. It is the law of energy. Energy causes many changes within the human body, as well as in the condition of the planet. Energy is always in a state of flux. The law of energy governs the changes in the human body, such as the aging process and health, and also, in the environmental context, such things as the climate, the seasons, and the tides of the ocean."

Pon said, "I think I understand about that one, Bhante."

"The second law is *bija niyama*, the law of germs and seeds, or you may like to think of it as the law of genetics. There are all kinds of seeds—each one producing a different plant or animal. The number and variety of plants and animals is so huge it is almost incomprehensible. However, there is only one kind of human seed that produces only one species of humans. The Buddha said, 'There is not among humans different kinds in the manner that they are found among other living creatures. Unlike other living creatures there is not among humans major differences in kind or species with regard to their eyes, ears, mouths, noses, lips, eyebrows, and even their hair—all are the same type.'² Do you understand this one, Pon?" I asked.

Pon replied, "Yes, you're saying that humans are all the same. There is really no reason for quarrels because of differences in race, color, caste, or gender."

"The third law is *kamma niyama*, the law of action; whatever one does, one reaps the consequences—either good or bad. There are many more explanations of the law of kamma, which we can discuss later."

"I would really like to understand that law better, Bhante. I look forward to your Dhamma talk another time," replied Pon.

"The fourth law is *dhamma niyama*, the law of nature, which governs everything in physical manifestation—including the earth in all its aspects. The surface of the earth rests on plates that sit on a moving mass of jelly-like substance. These plates move up against one another whenever there is pressure below the surface, and sometimes they move or shift to release this pressure, resulting in an earthquake. Earthquakes in the oceans can cause tsunamis."

"And what that means is that tsunamis are nothing more than naturally occurring phenomena," said Pon thoughtfully, waiting for me to continue.

"The fifth law is *citta niyama*, the law of the mind, the law that governs manifestation. The Buddha said, 'We create our world with our thinking. Either sorrow or happiness will follow us, depending on our thoughts.'"[3]

Pon had begun to think more broadly. "Bhante," he asked, "do these laws apply only to the human world?"

"No, Pon. The Buddha explained very clearly that the operation of these laws is not limited to this world; they actually apply throughout the universe. They affect every existing or future planetary system, and all forms of cosmic astrophysics. Disaster takes place from time to time because basic elements like water, earth, wind, and fire are always in a constant state of flux and can go out of balance.

"Buddhists do not believe that everything is due to kamma. They are aware of the roles played by other laws, including the laws of nature. Kamma is only one of the five laws that are in play at all times, each one exerting its influence as it may. Therefore, we must realize that our life experiences are not only due to the law of kamma.

"Each one of the five laws interacts constantly with one another. For example, extreme temperature (*utu niyama*) may influence the conditions of the mind (*citta niyama*). Or, strong willpower (*citta niyama*) may temporarily override the effects of negative environment (*utu niyama*) and the result of kamma (*kamma niyama*) in the case of natural disasters. In some instances kamma can actually override natural phenomena."

Pon was listening intently and with an expression of understanding.

I continued to explain, "I recently read in the *Daily News* from Sri Lanka a story about how a crocodile saved the life of an old man after the tsunami. According to the news item, the man was in the habit of allowing crocodiles to sunbathe on the embankment near his house, and he occasionally fed them. When the tsunami struck and he was washed into the river, he kept himself afloat for a few hours by grabbing onto a log that drifted toward him from out of nowhere. He clung onto this log for dear life as it floated *upstream* against the current. Eventually he drifted under a bridge where rescuers were grabbing people out of the water, pulling them to safety. It was only when the rescuers grabbed the old man and pulled him up that they all realized he wasn't floating on a log, but on the back of a crocodile that had saved him.[4]

"In this case, Pon, see how the results of wholesome kamma could even overcome natural phenomena? In this story, positive energy, compassion, generosity, and tolerance combined to allow the old man's good kamma to overcome disaster and provide a blanket of protection. It is essential for all human beings to cultivate compassion and show their kindness to all creatures, human or animal. This is especially important during times of crisis or extreme need—like a tsunami."

"Bhante, some people think that God was responsible for the tsunami. What do you think?" he asked.

"That's simply not true, Pon. It is a fallacy to blame external powers of any kind—natural or divine—for the tsunami or for any calamity that might occur. There is no one to blame, and nothing to blame on anyone. The tsunami disaster clearly demonstrated the flux of the earth's elements.

"However, this disaster is a reminder for us to think about our lifestyles and our relationship with nature. The world's scientific community has arrived at a consensus that the planet is undoubtedly warming. This has been attributed to carbon dioxide emissions from fossil fuel combustion and to deforestation. This warming will have dire consequences for the whole world.

Should we blame nature alone, or are we also contributing to this impending catastrophe?"

The Buddha said,

> It is according to the type of seed sown,
> What type of fruit is grown.
> Each one does the planting and reaping
> Good deeds bear the fruit of happiness, and
> Bad deeds bear the frut of sorrow.[5]

♦ ♦ ♦ ♦ ♦ ♦

8 ◆ Power of Meditation

I would like to tell you about an unusual and, as it turns out, a rather inspiring incident that took place in 1996. My friend Venerable Samahitho, a virtuous, kind, and skillful monk, was living at Wat Thai in the North Hollywood area of Los Angeles. Wat Thai was established in the early 1970s to serve the religious needs of the growing Thai community in Southern California. It is one of the largest Thai temples in the United States, and when you approach it from the street you would think you are in Thailand. It looks exactly like any one of the twenty-five thousand temples in that lovely country.

I often met Venerable Samahitho at international Buddhist conferences, interfaith dialogues in Los Angeles, or the meetings of the Buddhist Sangha Council of Southern California, for he was very active in the religious community and always eager to help others. Over the years we established a strong friendship, which made working together on mutual projects very pleasant. One day Venerable Samahitho asked me to deliver a talk at a meditation retreat at Wat Thai. It was there that I met an American gentleman named Dennis.

Dennis, who was at that time just over thirty years of age, was a successful computer engineer employed by a large corporation. Unfortunately, about two years before we met he had experienced a grand mal seizure and was later diagnosed with a cancerous brain tumor. He had had emergency surgery to remove the tumor, but it had already caused serious damage to the brain. As a result his motor skills were not in balance, which greatly affected his ability to walk or function normally. His memory was also impaired, and I remember him saying that he was experiencing frustration, major depression, and agitation. He was told that he had "organic brain syndrome," a chemical imbalance that adversely affected the central nervous system. He had lost a great portion of his memory, speech, and his ability to walk, unless assisted. He couldn't drink a glass of water without spilling it.

Although he had the best medical care available in the United States, the doctors informed him that there was no treatment for his condition and that he had no choice but to live with it and do the best he could. The only thing they could do for him was give him strong drugs to combat his increasing depression. The impairment of his physical and mental health meant that he had to give up his once-promising career, and before long his girlfriend left him.

Before his cancer diagnosis Dennis had been an experienced marathon runner. In the course of his marathon training, he had unknowingly developed a high degree of what we call in Buddhism "concentration of the mind." He had used this concentration to successfully compete against world-class runners.

In an attempt to deal with his brain condition and the resultant depression, Dennis started reading books on psychology and meditation, books that often referred to the strength that one could develop in the mind. Dennis was reminded of the strength he had developed in his own mind as a runner, and increasingly he began to seek out books on Buddhism and Buddhist meditation. One day when he saw the colorful green, red, and yellow tile roof of Wat Thai from the freeway he felt compelled to make a stop there.

Dennis's father was accompanying him that day, so together they entered Wat Thai and met Venerable Samahitho, the temple's primary meditation teacher. Venerable Samahitho encouraged Dennis, urging him not to give up hope in overcoming his illness, and that same day he taught Dennis a simple meditation technique that he could practice at home.

From that day forward Dennis practiced meditation diligently and, under the guidance of Venerable Samahitho, also became an *upasaka*, that is, a male devotee of Buddhism who observes the Five Precepts. When he attended meditation retreats at the temple he also observed the Eight Precepts.

Within three or four months Dennis began to notice an improvement in his mental and physical health, and the positive results from his meditation program continued as a year passed. About this time, Dennis decided to become an ordained monk, and he asked to be under the guidance of Venerable Samahitho, who agreed under one condition—that Dennis travel to Thailand to receive ordination.

Soon afterward Venerable Samahitho became the abbot of Wat Nak Prok in Bangkok where Dennis received ordination and was given the Buddhist name Dhammanissayo. Venerable Dhammanissayo remained in Thailand, serving as Venerable Samahitho's assistant and teaching meditation at the temple. In this setting he pursued the concentration of his mind and practiced *sati*, or mindfulness, with even greater vigor, and Venerable Samahitho arranged for him to further his studies on meditation by learning other techniques. Venerable Dhammanissayo thus went on to study the U Ba Khin method with Goenkaji (an Indian meditation master who was originally from Burma), as well as the Maha Sayadaw method with Burmese monks.

With meditation and mindfulness, Venerable Dhammanissayo was able to conceive of the mind and body separately and see the cause and effect of the thinking process. In time, he was actually able to reconnect the damaged components of his central nervous system through meditation; eventually the chemical imbalance in his brain was overcome, and he was able to begin leading a normal life. His health is now perfectly normal, and his memory has improved.

Venerable Dhammanissayo's meditation program demonstrates

one of many benefits from the practice, which was tradition-ally used only for spiritual development. Meditation can be very helpful in the management of stress, for instance, which may be caused by a combination of many factors in our daily lives. Per-haps we have to meet deadlines, pay bills, or our employers are putting demands upon us; it may be that we have been made anx-ious by unmindful words from family members, encountering road rage on the freeway, receiving demanding telephone calls, or experiencing health problems. In any case, one of the physi-ological effects of stress, from whatever source, is that it upsets our immune system. When the immune system isn't functioning properly, it cannot maintain and repair itself. In this way, stress can be a major cause for chemical imbalances, which impair the immune system and leave the body vulnerable to disease.

Meditation helps us manage our stress so it doesn't overwhelm us. It helps to create a naturally strengthened physical condi-tion that promotes self-healing, through the complete relaxation of both the body and the mind. Meditation leaves us with a feel-ing of deep contentment. During this state of contentment the mind can become purified; as meditators explore and experi-ence the nature of their bodies and minds in the course of their practice, they are able to "actually see" or understand themselves clearly, and they begin to live their lives according to that profound understanding.

The Buddha stated, "The original mind is luminous; it is *tar-nished* only by the *presence* of visiting defilements. The original mind is luminous; it is *untarnished* due to the *absence* of visiting defilements."[1] Our originally untarnished minds become pol-luted by thoughts of lust (*raga*), greed (*lobha*), hatred and aversion (*dosa*), and delusion (*moha*), which sometimes cause us to dwell on the negative, unpleasant aspects of life. When the mind is free from lustful, greedy, hateful, and delusional thoughts, it will be inclined to dwell on the positive or pleasant aspects of life. In this state we are able to see that all is well, that life is good, peaceful, and perfect. The practice that can eradicate defilements and lead to purity of mind is meditation.

The Buddha made use of two kinds of meditation techniques, *samatha* and *vipassana*. The *samatha* meditation technique was practiced by Siddhartha Gotama during the period before he became the Buddha and had been taught to him by his spiritual teachers.[2] It is a meditation practice that had been in use for a thousand years or more, which the Buddha modified for use to help meditators develop calmness—that is, serenity of mind through concentration.

For example, when we get angry and count to ten before we say anything, this is a form of *samatha;* we are concentrating on counting, and while we count the mind is able to calm down. Other practices of the *samatha* form are the use of a mantra (a word like "peace" or phrases like "I breathe in happiness, I breathe out happiness"), or counting from one to ten, then back to one, or counting breaths.

In this way the mind is given a simple task to perform, allowing it to stop the agitation caused by the bombardment of disturbing thoughts, such as anger, ill will, restlessness, and so forth. *Samatha* practice can help to bring serenity; the Buddha found these techniques could lead to deeper and deeper states of relaxation and peacefulness. But they did not lead to the knowledge of what caused suffering, nor did they eradicate the causes of suffering permanently.

Vipassana, or insight meditation, on the other hand, is a practice the Buddha discovered and taught as a tool for eliminating the mentally polluting thoughts that cause pain and lead to difficulties in our lives. It is also the tool given to us by the Buddha for cultivating wisdom (*panna*), the ability to understand the real nature of the world—and to see it for what it is and not for what we might think, want, or hope it is. The mind, once calm could be focused for the examination of one's physical, mental, and emotional states; insight, knowledge, and wisdom could thus be gained.

The practice of insight meditation leads to clear awareness, to experiencing the knowledge about "who" and "what" we think we are. By observing the thoughts that flow through our minds and the associated feelings that accompany those thoughts, we come to know our own selves. The Buddha said, "This path leads only to the purification of beings. It is for surmounting sorrow and lamentation, for eliminating pain and grief, for attaining the true way, for realizing Nibbana."[3]

The Buddha had his disciples begin practicing meditation by using the following phrases for the mindfulness of breathing. (By reading the following pairs of phrases slowly and carefully while sitting comfortably with your back straight you can experience a sense of well-being.)

I breathe in, experiencing the body breathing in.

>I breathe out, experiencing the body breathing out.

I breathe in, calming the body.

>I breathe out, calming the body.

I breathe in, experiencing contentment.

>I breathe out, experiencing contentment.

I breathe in, experiencing serenity.

>I breathe out, experiencing serenity.

I breathe in, experiencing the mental formation [thought].

>I breathe out, experiencing the mental formation [thought].

I breathe in, calming the mental formation.

>I breathe out, calming the mental formation.

I breathe in, experiencing the nature of the mind.

>I breathe out, experiencing the nature of the mind.

I breathe in, experiencing the uplifting of the mind.

I breathe out, experiencing the uplifting of the mind.
I breathe in, cultivating wholesome thoughts.

I breathe out, cultivating wholesome thoughts.
I breathe in, removing unwholesome thoughts.

I breathe out, removing unwholesome thoughts.
I breathe in, observing impermanence.

I breathe out, observing impermanence.
I breathe in, experiencing freedom from sensual addiction.

I breathe out, experiencing freedom from sensual addiction.
I breathe in, experiencing freedom from fear.

I breathe out, experiencing freedom from fear.
I breathe in, letting go of fear.

I breathe out, letting go of fear.[4]

With the use of these pairs of phrases the disciples were able to establish a sense of peacefulness within themselves. (These pairs of phrases could be recorded and listened to as a guided meditation.)

When the body and mind became calm and peaceful, the four foundations of mindfulness were contemplated:

1. contemplation of the body (*kaya*)—of its structure, function, and activities

2. contemplation of feelings and sensations (*vedana*)—and whether such feelings are pleasant, unpleasant, or neutral

3. contemplation of the mind (*citta*)—of the mind's activity, such as the arising and subsiding of thoughts

4. contemplation of Dhamma—the teachings of the Buddha, and especially of the Four Noble Truths (there is suffering, its origin, its cessation, and the path leading to the cessation of suffering)

The practice of insight meditation is not intended to have us *do* anything with what we perceive in ourselves, but rather it helps us to be able to truly *experience* ourselves without the running commentary of our thoughts. The Buddha said, "In your seeing, there should only be seeing; in your hearing nothing but hearing; in your smelling, tasting, touching nothing but smelling, tasting, touching; in your cognizing, nothing but cognizing."[5] When contact occurs through any of the senses, there should be no valuation. The evaluation of the contact as good or bad distorts the experience with old conditioning and reactions.

During meditation, observe the thought arising and fading away. The arising and fading away of another thought will follow. There seems to be an endless number of thoughts. Let the thoughts come and go without holding on or getting carried away with any one of them; without judging—good or bad, like or dislike. The experience is like watching a swiftly moving river. It is in this manner that we begin to understand the nature of our mind, by observing its contents, the accompanying feelings that arise with the thoughts, and its effect on the body (tension and breath).

Gradually with the practice of meditation, self-knowledge is gained, which brings with it the ability to solve difficulties. As it did for Dennis/Venerable Dhammanisayo, mastery of the meditation practice can completely transform one's life—from sickness to health, from darkness to light, and from unhappiness to happiness. The Buddha's teaching is the foundation for understanding, and a platform from which we can launch our own journey toward discovering our true selves.

The Peaceful Sage said
One having a single excellent night:

Relives not the past, for the past is gone.

Depends not on the future, for the future may not arrive.
Knows Mortality holds back Death for no one.

Recognizes that Now is when one must strive.
Sees and knows every present state
Consistently with energy,
Confidently and unwaveringly
Dwells thus during the day and through the night.[6]

♦ ♦ ♦ ♦ ♦ ♦

9 ◆ Getting to Know You, America

Early in its history, the United States opened its doors to immigrants from all over the world. This is a land of freedom and opportunity, where democracy is present in every corner of the country. In California, and especially in Los Angeles, which is considered a "melting pot," many nationalities have made it their home, bringing with them their distinct cultural identities.

Oftentimes people of ethnic origin prefer to live among themselves, forming small communities where they can live their lives as they did in their home country within the context of the larger American experience. In Los Angeles we have Little Tokyo, Little Saigon, Koreatown, Thai Town, Little India, Little Armenia, a mostly Mexican East L.A., and Chinatown, among others. Each of these ethnic areas has businesses that carry merchandise from the "homeland," as well as food items that have been imported to satisfy exotic palates. Within these communities—as well as throughout the greater Los Angeles area—we can find restaurants serving ethnic food from all over the world. In addition, each of the ethnic nationalities has established their own places of worship; there are congregations of various Christian denominations, Buddhist temples of different traditions, synagogues, mosques, Baha'i temples, Sikh temples, and so on—as many as there are ethnicities.

To a certain extent the creation of distinct, geographically located ethnic centers prevents individuals within those communities from absorbing each other's cultures and from absorbing the general American culture as well. It would be beneficial for all new immigrants to learn about American history and lifestyle before they come to this country. This will help them understand and better respect American culture from the very beginning of their American experience.

In the early 1990s, the image of Los Angeles was tarnished by a series of unfortunate, violent riots essentially due to poor cultural relations. They were triggered by the court's acquittal verdict in the case of a vicious attack by police officers on an African American man named Rodney King. The officers were acquitted in spite of the shocking brutality evident in a videotaped recording of the beating incident, which virtually everyone in the United States had seen.

There was another conflict in the city; this one arose because of the lack of understanding between the African American and the immigrant Korean communities. It was in this setting that a Korean neighborhood liquor store owner had shot and killed an African American teenage girl because she shoplifted a bottle of juice. The shop owner was convicted of voluntary manslaughter and the judge sentenced her to five years probation, rather than the sixteen years in prison that had been recommended by the jury. This verdict enraged the African American community, increasing the tension and resentment toward Korean store owners.

The early 1970s saw the beginning of the first big wave of Korean immigration to Los Angeles. Hard-working business-minded people immediately set up small, family-owned-and-operated businesses when they came to the United States. The whole family, including young and old members, worked in the business, and they all led frugal lives. Many families purchased "mom and pop" grocery stores in Koreatown and in the African American neighborhoods of South-Central L.A. as well. Their goal was to achieve the American dream of having a home, educating their children, and being financially secure. However, they clung fiercely to their own cultural traditions and showed no interest in studying English, which would have helped them communicate with non-Koreans. They usually relied on their children, who learned English in school, to act as translators.

As Korean businesses sprouted up seemingly everywhere, many African Americans believed that the Koreans had taken over their neighborhoods. The Koreans didn't hire anyone from the neighborhood, nor did they associate with any non-Koreans. They lived in an isolated world populated exclusively by transplanted Koreans, and there was no outside contact whatsoever. It seemed impossible for any kind of relationship or cultural understanding to develop due to the language and customs barriers.

Later, when the four police officers were acquitted in the Rodney King trial, it ignited years of resentment that had been building up in the African American community of South-Central Los Angeles. There was an outburst of anger lasting three days, which resulted in the looting and burning of many Korean businesses. Los Angeles is a very large city and it was difficult for the police to be everywhere at once. Korean shopkeepers went to their businesses to protect them from the looters who were roaming the city. Of course, not all of the looting was directed toward Korean-owned businesses, nor was it all committed by disgruntled African Americans. People intent on destruction and stealing in many areas of Los Angeles took advantage of the fragile situation, breaking into commercial premises and stealing merchandise. I saw many people who were not African American participating in the looting, and then smiling into the TV cameras as they came out of stores that were clearly not owned by Koreans.

Our temple is located within both the Korean and the African American communities. The house next door to the temple is owned and occupied by African Americans, and during the riots a fire broke out on their roof. With the help of all our neighbors (both Korean and African American) we managed to keep the fire under control by climbing onto our roof and hosing down their roof. Luckily the fire department arrived and completely put out the fire.

Because of our concern about the intense tension in the city during that time, arrangements were made for our temple's senior advisor, Venerable Dr. Ratanasara, to join me in visiting the community leaders from both groups. Korean monks whom I had known for a long time—the late Venerable Do Ahn Kim and Venerable Jin Gak Sunim—helped make plans for us to meet with the leaders of the Korean community. During our meeting, Venerable Dr. Ratanasara suggested strongly that the Koreans should learn English and learn about the culture and customs of this country.

One of the Korean members, Jim Moon, said, "We must maintain our customs and traditions even though we are living here. Our culture is over two thousand years old, whereas America is only a little over two hundred years old."

I replied, "Jim, it is good to maintain your traditions and show respect for your ancient culture; however, you must change your behavior when it comes to living in this country and doing business with Americans here."

"Oh, why is that?" he asked.

"I've been told that Korean women in your stores here never hand over change to a male customer. Instead, they put it on the counter. I've heard also that they don't look at the male customers' faces. Is this true?"

"Yes," he replied, "these are our customs."

"Then Jim, don't you see how this type of action automatically creates a misunderstanding? In this country it is the custom to make eye contact with customers, say 'thank you,' and put the change directly into their hands. If you don't do this, what you are doing is insulting that person, and the customer will probably never return. If we live in this country we must adapt to the customs here. Besides, you can see that it would be better for business."

Venerable Kim asked, "Bhante, what do you do as a Theravada monk if an American lady wants to hug you or shake your hand?"

"Of course, I'll extend my hand or accept the hug," I replied. "However, later on I will inform the lady about our cultural practices, and explain that monks should not have physical contact with members of the opposite sex."

Jim Moon was not satisfied. "Bhante, if we have to learn their customs, then they should learn ours, too."

"Jim, I will relate an amusing incident that happened to me on Halloween Day last year," I replied. "I went to see a patient at UCLA Medical Center, and many people approached me thinking that I was dressed for Halloween. I was wearing this saffron robe with a yellow cap and orange shoes. In fact, I was also carrying my saffron-colored bag. I can't blame them for their conclusions, but I had a hearty laugh and explained that this was my everyday wear."

I could tell by his face that Jim was still skeptical, so I told of another experience, this one being when I first came to America.

"When I was studying at Northwestern University in Chicago, my friends often invited me to their homes. Sometimes I would visit them at midday during the weekend. One day I visited a friend's family, and they were getting ready to have lunch. My friend's mother invited me to join them, but I politely declined. In Sri Lanka, when food is offered, the protocol is to refuse at first, then they insist, and then we can accept. I presumed that here in America the custom was the same. But it wasn't, so that day I went hungry. That incident taught me a very important lesson. We must learn to be aware of other people's cultural practices— especially American ones when we are living in America—and be flexible enough to use them for our survival and, most importantly, to be able to live together in harmony."

I left hoping that our Korean friends had been able to see what we were trying to tell them and that they would follow up with a willingness to learn more about American ways. Our next visit was to the African American group, whom we met in a Methodist church. One member of the group complained that the Koreans got loans from banks to help establish their businesses. Venerable Jin Gak Sunim, a Korean Buddhist monk who attended the meeting with us in order to represent his community, said that this wasn't true. He added that Korean businessmen form associations that help their members in getting businesses started. These associations actually provide financing and loans to the group members.

A man whom people addressed as Mr. Joseph, an African American businessman, was the next to speak. "The Koreans are rude," he complained. "They don't even greet us when we enter their stores. They don't put the change in our hands; they just drop it on the counter and expect us to pick it up. On top of that, they never even say 'thank you.'"

Venerable Jin Gak spoke up and said, "Please let me explain. These Koreans cannot speak proper English, so they are very shy about talking. In Korea the women usually do not look at the face of a male who is not an acquaintance, and they are raised to avoid physical contact. That is probably the reason why the change is put on the counter and not handed to the customer."

Mr. Joseph quickly added, "The Koreans think we're lazy, that we steal, and that we're rough."

Venerable Dr. Ratanasara replied, "Mr. Joseph, that is a total misunderstanding. The bodies of Koreans are small compared to you Americans; therefore, they assume you're all rough and tough. We must all work hard to show our true nature by practicing the willingness to try to understand someone who is different from ourselves."

Venerable Jin Gak said, "We Koreans admire Dr. Martin Luther

King, who followed Mahatma Gandhi's example of nonviolence. Mahatma Gandhi followed the Buddha's teaching of loving-kindness and compassion. Therefore, those of us who look up to King and Gandhi share a spiritual understanding, and I am positive we can overcome any misunderstandings that arise because of our differences in culture and customs."

The meeting ended on a friendly note, and it inspired all of us to try to be part of a solution that could bring the two communities together. We urged everyone to engage in more dialogue to achieve a better understanding.

About a month after our meeting, religious leaders from various traditions in Los Angeles organized a peace march to promote goodwill among all the city's ethnic communities. The march was held on Western Avenue. Starting at Hollywood Boulevard in Hollywood, we walked to Martin Luther King Jr. Boulevard in South-Central. The participants carried homemade banners depicting ideas and hopes for mutual understanding among the city's various ethnic groups. Many people wore the traditional dress of their native lands, and everyone had a wonderful, friendly attitude. We all held hands, forming a "bridge of friendship" that stretched for miles and miles while the peace march was in progress.

The Interfaith Coalition to Heal Los Angeles organized a public meeting in October 1993 focusing on the newly urgent goal of creating harmony among the different ethnic groups. Representatives from various religious traditions were invited to the First African American Methodist Episcopal Church, near Adams Boulevard and Western Avenue. I was honored to speak on behalf of the Buddhists, and here is what I said:

"I am happy to be here at this most important convention for peace. The Buddha taught us, 'Hatred is never overcome by hatred. By love is hatred overcome. This is the eternal law.'[1]

"Let us aim at creating a society where calm, peace, and understanding can prevail. In this time of turmoil, we of all faiths, all generations, all races and ethnic groups must speak with one voice for peace. Now is the time to build bridges of understanding between all the different peoples so that the anger, hatred, and ill will caused by ignorance can be eliminated.

"We should follow in the spirit of what Jesus Christ taught us about promoting peace in our lives; he says, 'Love your enemies and pray for those who persecute you, so that you may be sons of your Father, who is in Heaven.'[2]

"The time is right. In the spirit of all the religions we represent, as well as the modern teachers of nonviolence such as Mahatma Gandhi and Dr. Martin Luther King Jr., let us show others that we can, in the spirit of true democracy, have respect for our fellow human beings, work together, live together, and solve our problems together.

"Peace arises from within ourselves with noble thoughts, good actions, and faith in the ability of each individual to overcome hatred through love."

I then cited these lines from the Dhammapada:

Let us overcome the angry with loving kindness.
Let us overcome the wicked with goodness.
Let us overcome the miser with generosity.
Let us overcome the liar with truth.[3]

"Let us soften the hardest of hearts, bind one to another with cords of understanding, love and compassion. Let us destroy the barriers of class, creed, and race among the peoples of this earth. Let wisdom and compassion be the driving force of our actions. Let all living beings be treated with fairness; and let peace and harmony reign in our hearts."

At the end of the meeting the church choir came to the platform. All of the representatives joined hands, which was a surprising new experience for me, and we sang "We Are the World."

We swayed back and forth with our joined hands in the air. The church was filled with positive energy.

Later that evening I was inundated with phone calls because the peace meeting had been in the news on TV. My brother monks teased me, because in our tradition monks are not supposed to hold hands with females.

Even we Theravada monks have to face unfamiliar and some-times even uncomfortable situations where we have to go with the flow. That's how life is.

> One who is wise, of great wisdom,
>> thinks not with a view
>> to do harm either to oneself, or to another,
>> or to both alike.
> One thinks with a view to the benefit of self,
>> of another, of both self and another,
>> to the benefit of the whole world.
> Thus is one wise, of great wisdom.[4]

◆ ◆ ◆ ◆ ◆ ◆

10 • The Meditator

I met Joe, an American Zen monk, in India in 1973 at the Maha Bodhi Society in Calcutta. He had been ordained as a Mahayana Buddhist priest in the Vietnamese tradition at a temple in Los Angeles. Seeking to further develop his meditation techniques, he had gone to Japan to study with a famous *roshi*, a Zen master. After that, he went on to India to study under Anagarika Baruwa, who taught *vipassana* meditation at Buddha Gaya. Joe continued to practice the Zen form of meditation, but he combined it with the Theravada *anapanasati* form of meditation.

Joe was very intense and serious about meditation practice. He lived for three months at the Maha Bodhi Society, where I was also staying. I admired his rigorous practice; he usually sat for thirteen or fourteen hours a day. I was amazed at his perseverance, but he had an unusual personality, which made me curious about him. I wanted to find out what made him tick.

In our Sri Lankan tradition, meditation is not overly emphasized. Although I entered the Theravada order at the age of twelve, I had not spent a great deal of time meditating—usually only one hour each day. In our temple, the majority of our time was spent studying, memorizing Pali chants, and discussing the Dhamma with senior monks.

After a few weeks of being around Joe, I found it incredible that he could be so consistent in his meditation practice of fourteen hours a day. Even though he was a loner, I managed to become friends with him, and over time he convinced me that I should concentrate on developing my meditation practice. As a result, I took a course at Buddha Gaya for ten days, studying under the meditation master Goenkaji, who teaches the U Ba Khin tradition.

During this course I met two fellow students, lay people from America, who tried to convince me that I should visit America and share my knowledge of Buddhism. These conversations planted the seed in my mind of moving permanently to the United States and opening a temple. I also realized more clearly the true value of meditation, and how it could help the Western world. The Buddha, in one of his suttas, mentions that the study of Dhamma *and* the practice of meditation must be given equal time and attention in order for us to achieve true balance to our lives.[1]

Three years later I did, in fact, immigrate to America; and four years after that I founded a temple in Los Angeles, Dharma Vijaya Buddhist Vihara.

In 1980, I had the surprise of meeting Joe again. We were both at the funeral of Venerable Dr. Thich Thien-An, who had been one of Vietnam's leading meditation masters; Venerable Thien-An was the monk who had introduced the Vietnamese tradition to the United States. I learned that Joe was now living in Long Beach and was the instructor at a small meditation center.

We renewed our friendship, and in the mid 1990s he eventually started commuting to Los Angeles to lead meditation classes at my temple. I was happy to associate with Joe because he had indefatigable energy, which I admired. We often had discussions about meditation, since I disagreed with some of his extreme ideas about meditating, which included the practice of spending several days in seclusion, fasting; when Joe emerged from such extended meditations, he would appear physically weak. It was just after one such lengthy period of fasting that the following outburst occurred.

One day during a meditation class, in front of the other meditators, Joe announced that he did not believe in rebirth any longer and that now he only believed in reproduction. In fact, he said, he wanted to give up his meditation practice, get married, and have children. At this point I interrupted.

"It is too late," I said.

"Why?" he responded, shocked.

"You are over seventy years old," I replied. "You have spent most of your life meditating. You know little of what married life entails and you do not have the means to support a family."

He replied confidently, "Bhante, I have the stamina of a twenty-five-year-old man."

"Joe, I'm afraid you are on the wrong track. A meditator strives to eradicate all defilements. By meditating correctly, lustful desires, ill will, or hatred gradually fade away. The meditator becomes calmly energized and confident about his path."

"Bhante, your practice is superficial," he exclaimed.

"What do you mean?" I asked.

He calmly replied, "You give priority to loving-kindness meditation, and practically do nothing else. Do you believe you can eradicate all your defilements by practicing your way of meditation?"

"Joe, I am practicing what the Buddha taught in the early Buddhist text called the Anguttara Nikaya. It is called the Meghiya Sutta. In fact there are similarities in both your and Meghiya's character," I said with a smile.

"What is the Meghiya Sutta?" asked one of the other meditators.

"It is about a monk named Meghiya, who was, at the time, Buddha's assistant while they were staying at Calika, near the Kimikala River. One morning Meghiya accompanied the Buddha on his alms round. While they were returning to their camp, Meghiya noticed a beautiful and delightful mango grove and thought that it would be the ideal place to practice meditation.

"'Venerable sir, I have found a pleasant and delightful place to spend the day striving in meditation. May I go?' asked Meghiya.

"'Please wait until another monk arrives. If you go, I would be alone,' replied the Buddha.

"'But, venerable sir, you have already completed your task of enlightenment and have nothing more to strive for. I am still seeking to attain that which you teach. Please let me go to the mango grove to strive in my meditation,' pleaded Meghyia once more.

"'Meghiya, I have asked you to wait. Please do as I say,' was the Buddha's answer.

"Meghiya, not wanting to take 'no' for an answer pleaded again, 'Venerable sir, I implore you to let me go. You have already consolidated your achievement and have arrived at your exalted state. I still have much to attain. Please let me go to strive.'

"Finally, the Buddha said, 'If you wish to strive, please go to the place you feel is suitable.'

"Meghiya bowed to the Buddha and departed.

"He went to the mango grove and found a nice shady spot, then sat down with his back erect and began to meditate. His mind, however, refused to cooperate, and it assaulted him with distracting thoughts that horrified him because of their inappropriateness and unwholesomeness. Perhaps, since it was springtime and the young deer were abundant, Meghiya may have seen them mating. Witnessing this act may have caused him to have thoughts of sexual arousal, which, in turn, may have caused him to be ashamed of himself and feel guilty. Unfortunately, these feelings of guilt and shame may have made him quite angry with himself. After a while these angry thoughts may have led him to imagining himself hitting his head against a tree—an actual act of violence against himself.

"The occurrence of these three kinds of unwholesome thoughts completely took Meghiya by surprise. He had gone into the mango grove to meditate with faith, and he had the intention to strive for enlightenment. These thoughts, however, greatly disturbed him and caused him much grief.

"Then Meghiya went back to the Buddha and said, 'Venerable sir, I have failed in my attempt to strive for enlightenment. Almost as soon as I sat down in the lovely mango grove to meditate, the most unwholesome thoughts assailed me. First of all, I had the most outrageous thoughts about sex. Then I became angry at myself for these thoughts. The anger made me want to hurt myself and do something violent. Why did this happen?'

"'Meghiya, you asked me three times if you could go to the grove to meditate, and I told you 'no.' The reason I refused your request was that I knew quite well that you would have these sad results. Your mind is not yet mature enough to attain liberation. This is no fault of yours, but it is a condition you can improve with right effort and concentration.'

"The Buddha continued, 'The mind has to be mature in order to attain liberation, Meghiya. There are five conditions conducive to making the mind mature—like a ripened fruit that is sweet and ready to be enjoyed.

"'The first condition that would help to make the mind mature is close fellowship with a friend who knows what is good and wholesome, such as a wise teacher or a wise spiritual companion.

"'The second condition that aids in maturing the mind is for one to learn and practice good and wholesome behavior. The choosing of wise spiritual companions would be an example of virtuous behavior. Most of our learning and inspiration comes simply through watching how others do things.

"'The third condition is for one to engage in worthy conversation about the path to liberation. Conversation leading to mental clarity, understanding, calmness, contentment, comprehension, and insight to liberation is very valuable. In fact, if you are going to have conversation, have conversation about Dhamma; otherwise, remain silent. With wise spiritual companions, worthy conversation about Dhamma arises naturally.

"'The fourth condition is for one to make earnest and diligent effort to abandon everything that is unwholesome and to acquire everything that is wholesome. Don't give up on wholesome pursuits—including your pursuit of liberation. Wise spiritual friends can encourage us and guide us in our wholesome efforts.

"'The fifth condition is for one to gain deep insight into impermanence, and to realize that change is inevitable. With the understanding that everything in the world is constantly changing comes the knowledge that any unwholesome thoughts or actions that may arise can be abandoned and exchanged for wholesome thoughts and actions.'

"The Buddha told Meghiya, 'When a monk has a wise spiritual friend one can expect that he will be virtuous, that he will engage in conversation leading to mental clarity, that he will put forth effort diligently, and that he will develop the wisdom that will lead to the complete liberation from suffering.

"'When you have firmly assimilated these five conditions, and actually *live* them, then you should cultivate the following four practices:

Meditation on the foulness of the body for abandoning lust;
Meditation on loving-kindness for abandoning ill will;
Meditation on breathing for cutting off distracting thoughts;
Meditation on impermanence for eliminating the concept
    "I am."'

"Finally, the Buddha told Meghiya, 'When you have gained deep insight into impermanence, you will begin to understand the nature of your 'I am.' Once you understand that you are not this 'I am,' you must strive to eliminate the attachment to your *concept* of 'I am,' which includes thoughts of 'me,' 'my,' and 'mine,' and you will attain Nibbana in this very life.'"[2]

I looked at Joe. "Do you see now why I said that Meghiya reminded me of you?"

"Yes, Bhante, I see that you are comparing my eagerness and intensity to Meghiya's desire to sit in that mango grove, even though the Buddha knew it wasn't the right thing for him at the time. He persisted and did it anyway, in much the same way that I rashly decided to give up my practice and get married. It is true, I do not know much about married life. Perhaps I should work on the five conditions that are in the Meghiya Sutta, and I will continue to keep striving for enlightenment."

> Not understanding,
> The mind is easily led astray by thoughts
> Of no consequence.
>
> Understanding,
> The mind is easily disciplined,
> Ever watchful and ardent
> Those thoughts will no longer arise.[3]

◆ ◆ ◆ ◆ ◆ ◆

11 ◆ Spiritual Friends

Venerable Ananda, the Buddha's assistant and closest friend, once remarked to the Buddha, "Having a spiritual friend and companion is one half of living the holy life."

The Buddha replied, "No, Ananda, it is not half. The entirety of the holy life is spiritual friendship and companionship. Having a spiritual friend and companion enables you to develop and cultivate the Eightfold Path."[1]

The Buddha not only recommended having spiritual friends, he actually said it was *essential* to have spiritual friends if one was to succeed on one's spiritual path. He also said, "Having a good friend, having good companions, and being inclined toward good is the whole of spiritual life."

Ever since I came to California, I have been working with groups representing all Buddhist traditions: Tibetan Vajrayana practitioners; various sects of Chinese, Korean, and Japanese Mahayana practitioners; and Theravada practitioners from all countries. While I was studying at Northwestern University in Chicago, I used to practice Zen meditation with the Reverend Kubose; this was how I became involved in the Zen tradition. Reverend Kubose was a Jodo Shinshu priest who had long ago become interested in Zen meditation. He incorporated Zen meditation and practice into his daily life, and he taught it to his students. Reverend Kubose introduced me to his friend Roshi Tosa, a Zen master who lived in central California.

Whenever I had the time I joined Roshi Tosa at his meditation retreats, along with a large number of Western practitioners. I was happy to discover that the backgrounds of these practitioners were so diversified. The group included professionals of all kinds, craftsmen, tradespeople, members of the healing arts, and artists. Some group members were undertaking intensive training with Roshi Tosa to become Zen teachers themselves. These students, in particular, had great respect for their teacher.

Over the next few months my schedule at my temple in Los Angeles got busier and busier, and I no longer had time to attend Roshi Tosa's meditation retreats. After about a year's absence I was finally able to visit and I noticed that the number of students had dwindled considerably. Roshi Tosa was not in his quarters when I knocked at the door, so I asked Tony, his assistant, where he was.

Tony looked at the ground and didn't answer me right away, so I surmised that there was a problem.

"Come, Bhante, I'll take you to the vice abbot's office," he finally replied.

Tony introduced me to Reverend Miko, a Westerner who had been ordained by Roshi Tosa. We chatted for a while, and then I inquired, "Where is Roshi Tosa? I didn't see him in his room."

"Bhante, I have to share some bad news and some good news with you," he replied. "First, I will tell you the bad news. Our teacher has been accused of sexual misconduct and of being an alcoholic. It is a sad situation, since, as you know, he is a very good person and has done a lot for all of us."

"Where is he now?" I asked, surprised.

"Bhante, right now he is in an alcohol rehabilitation center in Orange County. The good news is that he is sober now, and we are bringing him home. We will have a welcoming ceremony next month on March 2, and I'm hoping you can attend. It is our every intention to take care of Roshi, because he has our highest respect."

"Yes, of course I'll come, Reverend Miko. It's hard for me to imagine that Roshi was an alcoholic. I've known him for years and I've never seen him drink," I replied.

"Bhante, let me explain what seems to have happened. Roshi was a dedicated man who, from the beginning, was determined to start a Zen meditation center here in California. In the early 1970s when he arrived in this country, he didn't have any money. During the day he taught meditation in a rented house, and at night he worked hard at a gas station to pay the rent. Eventually he and his wife saved enough money, and collected enough donations from students, to put a down payment on this property. It is literally true that Roshi and his wife built this place from scratch. They were the architects, the contractors, and the landscapers—as well as the laborers."

"But Reverend Miko, how did he wind up an alcoholic?" I asked.

"Bhante, in Japan, the average man drinks *sake* every day of his life. It's a long-standing tradition. When Buddhism first came there, they only practiced the first four precepts, and many Japanese monks drink. I'm guessing that Roshi developed the *sake* habit in Japan and brought it here with him. At some point it became an addiction. Even though some members of the congregation accused him of sexual harassment, I am positive he is not inclined that way. Probably, under the influence of alcohol, he could have become flirtatious and behaved in an inappropriate manner. We all decided that we should help him, and that's why we sent him to the rehab center. Furthermore, we've decided to protect him in the future by always having an assistant with him whenever he does his counseling work. We will take care of our teacher as our father."

"I am really amazed at your compassion. You are real spiritual friends to Roshi and to each other. I will definitely attend the welcome home ceremony."

"Thank you, Bhante; we look forward to seeing you. We would be most honored if you give us a special talk on 'spiritual friends' at that time."

On my trip back to Los Angeles I was thinking about how even spiritual teachers are sometimes led astray because of a lack of information. The meeting I just had with Reverend Miko definitely provided some food for thought. Along the barrier that divides the highway I noticed a sapling growing, probably from a seed that had been dropped by a bird. It was about a foot tall. I thought about how, if it were not removed, that small plant soon would grow into a large tree and damage the road. Likewise small habits can turn into addictions and damage our lives.

As scheduled, on March 22 I went to the *zendo* to welcome Roshi Tosa. The entrance to the Zen center was colorfully decorated with banners and flags—American, Japanese, and Buddhist. Outside the hall there were drummers and young children in their festive costumes, all waiting to give Roshi a big welcome. I thought about how pleased he would be when he arrived and saw these wonderful welcome preparations.

Roshi soon arrived amidst cheers, applause, dancing, and drumming. He was escorted to the *zendo*, where he bowed three times and offered incense and flowers to the Buddha. Then he seated himself at his customary place next to the Buddha statue. Reverend Miko started off the ceremony with a welcome speech. Afterward, he turned to me and announced that I would give a special talk on the topic of spiritual friends. I felt honored, and spontaneous words of appreciation flowed freely.

"Roshi," I turned toward him and said, "you are the luckiest person here, because you have such good spiritual friends. Your congregation solved a sensitive problem in a quiet, skillful manner. They proved themselves to be sincere spiritual friends who came to your rescue when you needed them. They have understood the essence and extent of the Buddha's compassion."

I turned to the audience and said, "I appreciate the wisdom all of you demonstrated by your concern for your teacher. On his behalf, I thank you for your kindness in restoring him with honor.

"I have to confess that if I, or any other South or Southeast Asian monk had landed in a similar uncomfortable situation, we would have been torn to pieces and discarded for good. There would be no returning for me, or for any others in our tradition—no matter who we were, or what we had accomplished.

"All of you present here today have paid great tribute to the Buddha, and to Buddhism itself, with your exemplary treatment of your fine teacher. In the early Buddhist texts, the Buddha states, 'Good friendship, good companionship, good comradeship . . . is the entire spiritual life.' The Buddha goes on to say that spiritual friends are not only a necessity for living a good life, but they are also a necessity if one is to attain liberation. Without spiritual friends, liberation is usually impossible.[2]

"For our spiritual progress it is of the utmost importance that we carefully select good friends and companions. Since our friends have a dramatic influence on our lives, if we choose the wrong people to associate with, we could wind up on the wrong path. The Buddha clearly realized this and talked about the vital importance of having a *kalyanamitta*, or a spiritual friend.[3]

"In the Theravada tradition," I said, "at the conclusion of all our services, we chant this verse in Pali:

Imina punna kammena Mame bala samagamo
Satam samagamo hotu Yava nibbana pattiya

"This translates as:

By virtue of wholesome acts may I never associate with fools,
And may I associate only with the wise until I attain
    Nibbana.[4]

"A spiritual friend will influence and guide you along the Noble Eightfold Path, which leads to the end of suffering," I continued. "Furthermore, the Buddha has said that a spiritual friend will do everything in his power to stop you from doing anything that might cause you or anyone else to suffer. He also said that associating with a spiritual friend can help you develop your faith, acquire good character, increase your knowledge, encourage you to be generous, and develop a good understanding of human nature.[5]

"If we associate with a person who is spiritually developed, then we will also aspire to travel the spiritual path.

"In the Sigalovada Sutta, the Buddha warned us about four types of people who appear to be friends, but who are actually the opposite. The Buddha tells us to avoid these false friends. The first type is someone who only takes and never gives. The second type is someone who only talks and never acts. The third type is someone who flatters you to your face, but talks behind your back. The fourth type is someone who encourages you to waste your money.

"In the same sutta the Buddha talks about the four types of people who are true and loyal friends. The first of these is a friend who is helpful, protecting you and your property, providing a refuge in troubling times, or offering the means to help you conduct your business.

"Another type of friend is one who is the same in prosperity and adversity, sharing and keeping secrets with you, not abandoning you during times of trouble, and even putting themselves at risk for you.

"The third type of friend is one who gives good counsel, keeping you from doing wrong, encouraging you to do good, sharing profound thoughts with you, and guiding you along a spiritual path.

"One last type of friend is one who understands and sympathizes, sharing your sorrows, rejoicing in your successes, restraining others who speak ill of you, and praising others who speak well of you.

"To sum up, spiritual friends will never let each other down, just as you have taken care of your teacher in his time of need. I'm sure that you can count on him to be there when you need him. I would like to acknowledge you, my spiritual friends, for looking after Roshi."

Roshi never again touched *sake*. Tirelessly, he preached and taught others to abstain from intoxicants and to live virtuous lives. Even though some Japanese Buddhist traditions only practice four of the Five Precepts, Roshi, from the time of his return home, instructed his students to keep all five—including the abstention from alcohol.

Over the years, the attendance at Roshi's *zendo* increased and even surpassed its previous numbers. His students remained faithful to him until the end, and they looked after him lovingly as their own father until he passed away.

> When journeying through life,
> Accompany the prudent and wise
> Who live a wholesome life.
> Thus you can overcome obstacles
> To live mindfully and happily.
>
> When journeying through life,
> Unable to find the prudent and wise
> Who live a wholesome life,
> Better to go on alone
> Avoiding troubles caused by the foolish.
>
> Live alone and avoid doing wrong.[6]

◆ ◆ ◆ ◆ ◆ ◆

12 ◆ Virtue

Mr. Ngyuen Lee lived in Vietnam before the war, where he met the Venerable Narada Maha Thera, a Sri Lankan monk. Although Ngyuen was born into a Mahayana Buddhist family, he became a Theravada Buddhist due to Venerable Narada's influence.

Venerable Narada—himself a devoted, educated, and renowned Buddhist scholar, the author of many Buddhist books, and an authority on Theravada Buddhism—gave Ngyuen the Buddhist name of Soma at his initiation as an *upasaka* (a male devotee who has taken the Five Precepts). Soma Upasaka was so devoted to this commitment that he liked to be called by his Buddhist name. He immigrated to the United States in 1975 after the fall of Saigon.

I happened to meet Soma Upasaka at the Vietnamese Theravada temple in Pomona, a town about thirty miles east of Los Angeles. After that, he frequently came with his family to visit my temple on Crenshaw. For some reason, Soma was obsessed with the Vinaya rules that are the guidelines for Buddhist monks to follow. In that regard, one of his pet peeves was making sure that any monk within his circle would not consume even a morsel of food after twelve o'clock noon.

One day he organized a lunch at his home in Pomona for the monks of my temple and the monks from the Vietnamese Theravada temple. Unfortunately for me and the Dharma Vijaya monks, traffic prevented us from reaching his home until about 11:55 a.m. As we walked in, I explained the reason for our late arrival, and the Vietnamese Sangha members asked us to join them at the table without delay. By the look on his face, which darted back and forth to the clock, I knew that Soma was disappointed that we had arrived a bit too late to suit his strict schedule.

The Vietnamese monks had wanted to wait for our arrival to begin the meal, but Soma insisted that they start their lunch at 11:30 in order to finish before noon. The monks couldn't refuse his strong desire to begin serving them on time, so they consented and started eating.

Just as we sat down, the clock struck noon. Soma, whose eyes and ears were glued to the clock, ordered his wife and children to remove the food from the table. He asked them to remove our plates as well. We had hardly even had a chance to taste the delicious-looking food, but since Soma believed so strongly that monks shouldn't eat after noon, our meal disappeared in a flash.

I could see the look of embarrassment on his wife's face—and even on the faces of the children. Soma's teenage son said, "Dad, they haven't had lunch yet. Why did you take their food away?"

"Monks can't eat after noon, Jason. We have to respect that," was Soma's stern reply.

Soma then started to explain how virtue plays an important role in the Vinaya. He said that if we offer *dana* to monks who practice the Vinaya correctly, then those who offer the food can also attain full enlightenment.

Soma's wife, Minam, said, "Bhante, please forgive my husband's rudeness and strange behavior. I am so sorry he took your food away. Please explain to us exactly what the Buddha intended when he made his rules about lunchtime. I can't believe he would agree with having food removed because his Sangha members showed up five minutes late."

Soma started to say something in his defense, but his wife gave him a look that told him to remain silent.

"I am glad you asked me this question, Minam. With the permission of the Sangha members present here, I will explain what the Buddha said about monks consuming food.

"First of all, during the Buddha's time, there were no clocks as we know them today. Time was measured by the position of the sun. When the sun was directly overhead that was called midday, or noon. Noon isn't exactly at the same time every day.

"The monks originally went out to receive alms three times a day. This became a burden on the laity, as well as on the monks, and unpleasant experiences resulted for both. In the winter, people would keep their doors closed. Since they didn't have indoor plumbing, at night when they washed their dishes they would throw the water out the window, sometimes hitting a passing monk. Also, a figure walking after dark would be mistaken for a hungry ghost. After a while the lay people came to the Buddha and asked him to tell the monks not to come to their homes in the evening. The Buddha considered their request and recommended to the Sangha that they receive alms only once a day, before noon.

"He said, 'Bhikkhus, I eat once a day and I enjoy health, strength, and I am able to meditate in comfort. I suggest that you also eat once a day. Then you too will enjoy health, strength, and be able to meditate well.'

"When Venerable Bhaddali heard this, he told the Blessed One, 'Venerable sir, I do not want to eat only one meal a day; if I do, I might have worry and anxiety.'

"The Buddha responded, 'Then, Bhaddali, eat only a part of your meal and save a part to eat later. By eating in that way you will maintain yourself.'[1] In other words, the Buddha wasn't as strict as you think he was about the eating rules for monks. He was mainly concerned about the monks disturbing the laypeople in any way—especially disturbing their faith by doing something inappropriate. However, the Buddha strongly urged the monks to eat one meal a day since they don't do any physical labor. He knew that three meals a day might make them fall asleep, which would curtail their meditation practice. He also knew that they would gain weight and become unhealthy."

Soma seemed to understand what I was trying to get across to him. He even asked me to talk some more, this time about virtue.

I said, "The Buddha never gave a sermon when people were hungry. He knew that it would affect their ability to listen. Please, Soma, you and your family finish your food and then I'll give you the talk you requested."

Soma nodded his head, and I could sense that he felt bad about taking away our food before we could eat it. Anyway, he and his family went back to their meal and then called us to come into the dining room when they were finished.

We went into the dining room, and Soma handed me and each of the Dharma Vijaya monks a mug of hot broth. I knew that this was his way of demonstrating that he had learned a lesson and that he regretted his ill manners.

We finished our broth, and then I began. "Developing virtue, or *sila*, is the most important preliminary requirement to ensure our spiritual progress. *Sila* is the foundation of all meritorious deeds, because without virtue there is no merit. On the surface, *sila* is morality, good conduct, and the observance of precepts. However, beneath the surface, *sila* is much, much more. *Sila* is the root of *samadhi*, or concentration; therefore without *sila*, there can be no concentration; with *sila*, concentration can be developed. *Samadhi*, concentration, is developed only through the practice of meditation, which is also the method for cultivating *sila*.

"Furthermore, without *samadhi*, there can be no *panna*, or wisdom. *Sila*, *samadhi*, and *panna* are completely interrelated and are developed at the same time. Once these three characteristics are developed to a sufficient degree, then spiritual advancement can proceed. When they are developed to their full capacity and strength, then enlightenment takes place.

"If one wishes to achieve satisfactory results from one's meditation practice, one must at least practice the Five Precepts, the most basic training rules for virtue.

"*Sila* can be divided into two categories: *caritta sila*, or virtue that is based on developing certain practices; and *varitta sila*, virtue that is based on avoiding certain practices. One category is positively directed, the 'dos'; and the other is negatively directed, the 'don'ts.'[2]

"Examples of *caritta sila* are such activities as offering hospitality to visitors, taking care of one's parents and family, making offerings to the Buddha, keeping one's home clean and organized, and keeping one's body and mind clean.

"Examples of *varitta sila* are included in the Five Precepts: do not kill, do not steal, do not commit sexual misconduct, do not lie, and do not take intoxicants. Other 'don'ts' would be, for instance: do not slander others, do not speak harshly, do not babble foolishly, do not be avaricious, do not have ill will, and do not hold wrong views.[3]

"According to Buddhism, suffering follows one because of one's unwholesome deeds, whereas happiness follows one because of one's wholesome deeds.[4] Therefore, in this respect the main task in gaining happiness and eliminating suffering is to avoid immoral deeds (*varitta sila*), and to do good moral deeds (*caritta sila*), as prescribed by the Buddha. Such behavior is called individual moral conduct.

"Developing *caritta sila* helps to organize one's life for the benefit of both the individual and society. The Buddha advised his disciples not only on how to conduct themselves, but also on how to live an organized, clean life in a pleasant environment. The disciples had to follow a strict code of ethics that would enable them to live a harmonious life; this included keeping their living quarters clean and neat, and also maintaining their personal hygiene.

"Let me tell you of my own experience with trying to balance *caritta sila* and *varitta sila*. Back in 1970 I was teaching at Vidyodaya University in Gangodavila, Sri Lanka. I took a group of my students on a pilgrimage to see Mihintale, a one-thousand-foot mountain that Arahat Mahinda visited when he brought Buddhism to Sri Lanka. Arahat Mahinda was the son of Emperor Asoka of India and lived in the third century B.C.E.

"While we were climbing the 1,840 steps to the top of the mountain, a group of teenage girls were walking just ahead of us. As we neared the top, the girls began fooling around, laughing and pushing each other. One girl lost her balance and started to fall. As I was the closest to her, I reached out with both arms to keep her from falling. Behind me and my group of students were some old ladies who immediately began to criticize me for touching the teenage girl.

"One of them said to me directly, 'You are breaking a Vinaya rule, young monk. You may not touch a woman!'

"I replied to her, 'Did you want me to let her fall down the mountain and die? If I hadn't caught her, that's what would have happened!'

"The old woman could not answer me, and she turned away, embarrassed."

I asked Soma, "What do you think the Buddha would recommend in a life-or-death situation like that? Is it more important to do a good deed, or avoid breaking a rule of conduct?"

"It is far better to do a good deed, Bhante," he replied.

Jason, Soma's son, asked, "Bhante, do laypeople have to follow these rules?"

I replied, "Jason, monks are striving for the highest level of wisdom and compassion. Therefore, Buddhism is a religion, a philosophy, and a way of life to attain these goals. But these goals are not only for monks; laypeople can also have these goals. The Buddha gave us certain precepts to help both monks and laypersons organize their lives—both internally and externally. It is my experience that when one's physical environment isn't well organized, a person can't think properly or with correct perspective. The full potential of an individual can only be seen when one's life is organized within and without.

"The Buddha gave his son, Samanera Rahula, the surest test for determining if something was moral or immoral. He said, 'If you wish to do a certain action, first take a look and decide if it will harm you, others, or both. If the action is likely to cause suffering, don't do it.'[5]

"The Buddhist perspective of morality is given in a nutshell in this verse from the Dhammapada: "To keep away from all wrongdoing, cultivate good, and purify one's mind is the advice of all Buddhas.'"[6]

At the end of this talk, Soma and his family came before me and the other monks and paid their respects. We chanted for them and tied the blessed string around their wrists.

It wasn't too long before Soma and his wife came by the temple one evening. Soma approached me in the kitchen with a big pot. "Here is some clear, Vietnamese vegetarian broth for you, Bhante Piyananda, just in case someone else grabs your food."

We all laughed and remembered the day Soma had been so strict in the enforcement of Vinaya rules. "You helped me learn a very important lesson that day, Bhante. Lightening up on rules and learning to enforce them with love has helped bring more peace and harmony to our family. We are all grateful to you."

Soma and his family continue to visit the temple, and every now and then they offer *dana* at breakfast or lunch.

> One who abides in loving-kindness,
> Who is delighted in the Teaching of the Buddha,
> Attains the state of calm,
> The happiness of stilling the conditioned things.[7]

♦ ♦ ♦ ♦ ♦ ♦

13 ◆ Mistaken Identity

I have noticed during my thirty-two years of spiritual counseling certain patterns that keep repeating themselves in the people I meet. Most of these patterns have to do with three things: attachments of one kind or another, the ego's need to feel "in control," and mistaking the motivation behind one's thoughts or actions. This is the unconscious mistake of allowing oneself to be deceived by one's own thoughts. These patterns result in negative thoughts, feelings, or actions—such as not taking responsibility for one's self and the resulting feelings of anger, frustration, and jealousy. These negative patterns could easily be avoided by following a practice of observing, cleaning, and clearing the mind of those troublesome thoughts.

The Buddha talked about *vanchaka Dhamma*—how thoughts can be misidentified. This can be very dangerous because the mind can actually fool itself into thinking that an unwholesome act or thought is actually a wholesome act or thought.

The story of Tanya is a perfect example of this kind of mental deception. Tanya was an attractive, well-dressed Thai lady in her mid-thirties whom I had known for nearly five years. During that time she would often come and talk to me about suspicions she had about her boyfriends. Her pattern was to blame her boyfriends for their relationship problems and then break up with them, after accusing them of infidelity. She did this with one boyfriend after another, and the unfaithful acts she suspected were sometimes only in her imagination. She also claimed to be psychic, which could be dangerous for friends and relatives who believed her.

One day Tanya came to the temple with her friend Ruja, another Thai lady, who was in her mid-twenties. Ruja wanted to talk to me about her boyfriend, Terry. Terry was an American who was completing his master's degree in engineering at San Diego State. Tanya had told Ruja that she had psychic powers. She also told her that Terry was seeing other women behind her back. Ruja took Tanya at her word because she truly believed her friend was psychic. After a while Ruja had become completely obsessed by the idea that Terry was being unfaithful. She told me that she could no longer sleep and was losing weight as a result of her worries.

Ruja said, "I just can't trust Terry, Bhante. He lives so far away and I can't see what he's doing. I've asked him to move up to Los Angeles, but he refuses."

"Ruja, I thought you said that Terry was working on his masters degree? Why don't you move to San Diego if you are so concerned about him," I suggested.

"I can't, Bhante. I'm in my last year at university, and moving is out of the question until I graduate."

Tanya spoke up with excitement. "Bhante, why are all men cheaters? I don't trust any of them."

I turned to Tanya and said, "Have you been telling Ruja that you have psychic information about Terry that might have caused her to believe Terry is unfaithful?"

Tanya seemed surprised at my question, and she said, "Bhante, I've told you before that I am very psychic. I can't help it if I am given information about others that I am supposed to share with them. I had a dream about Ruja and Terry, so of course I told her about it. She's my friend. I only want to help her!"

"How do you know for sure that your psychic feelings are genuine, Tanya? You are bringing a very serious accusation against Terry, and you are causing Ruja to lose sleep."

"I know it's true from my own experience, Bhante," she replied.

"You mean your experience with your own boyfriends?"

"Yes, Bhante, I've told you before about how my boyfriends were always cheating on me."

"Don't you see that you may be projecting your own unfortunate experiences onto your friend? You may have dreamed about *your* boyfriend and misinterpreted it as being about Ruja's. You know, Tanya, the Buddha often talked about the mind and the tricks that thoughts can play on it."

"No, Bhante, there aren't any tricks. What I dream is real," she replied.

"Tanya, there is a saying, 'The ugliness we see around us is a reflection of our own thoughts.' Could you possibly be seeing things about your life that you don't like? Are you transferring them to Ruja? Your past problems, and Ruja's present one, seem to be far too much alike to be a coincidence."

"Bhante, what do you mean by 'projections'? Everything I've told you—and Ruja—is the truth," she exclaimed emphatically.

"The Buddha taught us to be constantly on guard with our minds: To watch each and every thought very carefully. He wanted us to be aware of the possibility that our mind wasn't always seeing the truth, and to be aware of mental disguises. Did you know, Tanya, that the thoughts in your mind are only real to you? And the thoughts in Ruja's mind and my mind are only real to us? Sometimes our minds can play tricks on us. The mind can make us think we are doing something good when in reality we are doing something very destructive. The mind can accept a bad thought in the disguise of a good thought and be completely fooled," I explained.

"Let me tell you a story that may make this clearer for both of you," I began. "Long ago there was a great teacher who was known for his deep meditation. One day after meditating he pointed to one student, Ling, and said, 'When I was meditating I saw you clearly as a Buddha sitting on a lotus flower.'

"Ling grinned sheepishly and said, 'I saw you in my meditation, too, Master.'

"'Please tell us,' replied the master.

"Ling hesitated before replying softly, 'I saw you as a pig sitting in cow dung.'

"One of the other students stood up and began shouting at Ling. The master said, 'Don't scold him. He is only describing what he saw. He didn't mean to be disrespectful. The truth is, my mind is clean like the Buddha. I saw Ling as a Buddha. His poor mind is full of defilements. He saw me as a pig sitting in filth. It's just like a man putting on a pair of green-tinted glasses: When he looks out at the world everything is green. If he changes them for a pair of red-tinted glasses, everything will be red. This is the same as the mind, which has filters. If there are defilements everything will look defiled. If it is pure and clean, then everything will appear as the Buddha.'

"Ling bowed before his master and said, 'Please teach me how to get rid of the defilements in my mind, Master. I no longer wish to see the world through my mind's dirty filters.'

"The master said, 'You have already taken the first step, Ling, by seeing this flaw in your mind. The Buddha said "The fool who knows he is a fool is that much wiser. The fool who thinks he is wise is a fool indeed."'

"Tanya, if you get into the practice of watching your mind very carefully you will be able to see the thoughts that defile it. Eliminate them as they arise. You don't need to suppress the unclean thoughts. Just notice them, and ignore them. They will soon cease bothering you. You will be able to see things as they really are."

Tanya considered this carefully and said, "I studied psychology in college, Bhante, but mental deceptions were never explained to me in this way."

"I'm glad you are beginning to understand, Tanya. I think your mind was looking through the filter of anger," I explained further.

"These angry thoughts were putting on a disguise. They were deceiving you when you told Ruja about Terry. As a result, Ruja has been suffering unnecessarily."

"It's true, I have been thinking that most men will cheat on their girlfriends. I suppose that belief is not necessarily true. I'm very sorry if I've hurt your relationship, Ruja," she responded.

"That's okay, Tanya. I know you thought you were looking out for me. I understand," said Ruja.

"Tanya, what you did is because your mind was deceived. Without your being aware of it, angry thoughts had filled it. It caused Ruja distress. It caused you to suffer as well. Do you think this could have been the case with some of your previous boyfriends? You thought they were cheating on you, but maybe they were not," I suggested carefully.

"Maybe, and maybe not—I will never know for sure. But I do know that the first one I told you about, Tom, *was* cheating on me. I actually caught him with another woman!" Tanya was really getting angry and upset reliving these memories.

"Tom is in the past, Tanya, and this is now. Whenever you think of unpleasant things from the past, you bring them into the present and spoil the now. You have had a great deal of pain in the past. I'm trying to help you see that much of it is because you let your mind be deceived. The thoughts of the past continue to cause you pain. Once you understand this, Tanya, you don't have to be attached to those memories. You can let go of the pain," I continued.

"Now that you put it that way, Bhante, I'm sure you're probably right about my past. I might still be in a relationship with one of the young men I used to go out with if I hadn't accused all of them of infidelity and ended the relationships. My first boyfriend, Tom, was unfaithful, and because of him I assumed all the rest were too. This could have been my mind being fooled by thoughts in disguise. I'm alone now, and it's my own fault," exclaimed Tanya.

"Don't feel bad, Tanya. Now you know this pattern from your past. I'm sure you will someday have another boyfriend, and you still have a chance of having a wonderful relationship. Just don't dwell on the past. Be completely open to the present moment and see what happens."

I turned to Ruja, "I think you can put aside your doubts about your boyfriend. It seems that Tanya has been projecting her own thoughts of anger and fear onto your relationship with Terry. She didn't understand her thought pattern until now, so you can't blame her for trying to be a good friend. Why don't you give Terry a chance and see for yourself if there is any reason to doubt him?"

Ruja smiled at me and said, "I will take your advice, Bhante, because I really love him. I think we can have a future together."

"Why don't you come and see me again. Bring Terry with you. I'll speak to both of you together. You can make a new beginning."

Ruja agreed and said she would bring Terry the following weekend.

The two ladies bowed and paid their respects to the Buddha statue. I noticed, however, that Tanya still seemed bothered by something. She gave me a smile, and the two of them left the temple.

The next day Tanya showed up at the temple alone. By the look on her face I knew she was very upset.

"Tanya, I can tell something is the matter. What's wrong?" I asked.

Tanya frowned and said, "I don't want Ruja and Terry to come to see you at the temple alone. I want to be there with them."

"Then why don't you come with them, if it is alright with Ruja," I replied.

"Ruja doesn't want me to come," she said with anger.

"Then what's the problem, Tanya? There is nothing wrong with Ruja bringing Terry to the temple without you."

"I brought Ruja here the first time, and she should only contact you through me. I don't want her coming here without me."

"It sounds like you have control issues to work through, Tanya. Ruja has every right to act on her own. Yesterday we discovered how your mind repeatedly deceives you about your boyfriends. Today you are exhibiting another pattern of mental deception: the need to control the people around you. This is just another reason for your suffering, Tanya. Once you can release this pattern of behavior, you can be happy. You have no right to get angry with Ruja for wanting privacy when she visits me. This is nothing for you to be concerned with," I explained firmly.

Tanya paused to reflect for a moment. She finally said, "Yes, Bhante, somehow I think I enjoy controlling others. I think I know what is best for them. I feel that if they don't listen to me then they will suffer. Besides, I don't think Terry is right for Ruja. He is an American boy, and she doesn't understand him."

"What's wrong with Ruja having an American boyfriend? How do you know she doesn't understand him?" I replied.

"I just know it—I'm psychic, remember?"

"Then you must also remember what we discovered yesterday about your mental deceptions, Tanya. Are you sure this is valid psychic information? Are you just jealous that Ruja has a good relationship and you don't?"

Tanya couldn't answer me. I continued, "It is very easy to mask your negative feelings of jealousy under the guise of saying you psychically know what's best for your friend. You might be fooling yourself, Tanya, and not only that but you are hurting Ruja."

"Do you think I am jealous, Bhante?"

"You may or may not be jealous, Tanya; that is for you to investigate and decide. The Buddha warns us about how such unwholesome feelings as jealousy, anger, or revenge disguise themselves as wholesome feelings such as compassion and love.

"Causing trouble for others and for yourself is an unwholesome activity, Tanya. The Buddha states, 'When you know for yourselves that certain things are unwholesome (*akusala*) and wrong and bad, then give them up . . . And when you know for yourselves that certain things are wholesome (*kusala*) and good, then accept them and follow them.'"[1]

"You're right, Bhante. You've shown me how I really need to be on my guard so my mind isn't deceived any more. I never knew that thoughts could be so subtle in their deceptions. I also see that there is no need for me to come to the temple with Ruja and Terry. Let them have their privacy."

"I'm glad you understand, Tanya," I responded. "If you study the Dhamma carefully you will find many instances where the Buddha describes the nature of the mind and the consequences of incorrect thinking. He said, 'Neither your parents nor anyone else can do you greater good then your own well-directed mind.'"[2]

"Thank you, Bhante, for your patience with me."

"Also, please remember to be very careful when you give psychic advice to others, Tanya. Make sure your mind is not being deceived. A great deal of meditation practice and cultivating a pure mind is needed to develop psychic ability. I'm not doubting the ability you say you have, but please make sure that you learn how to distinguish your own thoughts from your psychic guidance. Until you are sure, you may want to keep your psychic information to yourself. If you really want to develop your psychic abilities, you need to have a strong foundation in loving-kindness, compassion, appreciative joy, and equanimity. In order to develop these four sublime states, you need to consistently practice meditation. You will then be able to grow your psychic abilities to truly help others. You will also find that you are a much happier person."

"Yes, Bhante. I can see I should probably start coming to meditation class so you can guide me in this process." She left the temple that day in a positive frame of mind.

As they promised, Ruja and Terry came to see me and have been working successfully on their relationship. Tanya continues to meditate and has a new boyfriend.

He abused me.
He mistreated me.
He defeated me.
He robbed me.
Live with such thoughts and you live in anger.

He abused me.
He mistreated me.
He defeated me.
He robbed me.
Release such thoughts and you banish anger for all time.[3]

♦ ♦ ♦ ♦ ♦ ♦

14 ✦ Overcoming Gambling

Sanjiv, his wife, Pavitra, and their two daughters were longtime and frequent visitors to my temple. Over a period of two years, however, I had been hearing rumors that Sanjiv had a severe gambling problem. I decided it might be time to confront him about it.

"Sanjiv, I've been hearing stories about you borrowing money from temple members and never paying it back. They say you are a gambler."

"I never borrow money, Bhante. Whatever you have heard is nothing but lies," was his reply.

I looked at Sanjiv's face and immediately knew that he was not telling the truth. Just at that moment Pavitra stepped into the room to join us. "I overheard what you just asked my husband, Bhante, and, unfortunately, what you said is true," she said. "My husband has good qualities, too. He never drinks, he loves our children, and he never abuses me physically or verbally. Yet, the mental stress I am under because of his gambling habit makes life with him very difficult."

Sanjiv was quick to defend himself. "Well, all right, I admit that I do gamble, Bhante, but it's all for my family's benefit. When I win, I will buy a nice house, give my children a good education, see to their needs, and provide everyone with a comfortable life."

Pavitra interrupted and said, "How dare you say that it is for our benefit, when we are the ones who are made to suffer because of your gambling! It's better to be on the streets than to use money you win from gambling. As if there were any winnings in the first place—you've been gambling for over twenty years and have nothing!"

I could tell that this husband and wife were both experiencing a great deal of stress and were unable, at this point, to cooperate with one another. I felt sorry for the whole family, because obviously they were living in a world of despair. I was also determined to help them, and I suggested counseling to Sanjiv.

"What kind of counseling could help *him*, Bhante? He even took the money from my children's piggy banks and gambled it away," Pavitra said hotly. I could hardly believe her words, describing that her husband had stooped so low.

"You can clearly see that gambling is an addiction like drugs, womanizing, or alcohol," I responded. "Any addiction ultimately destroys the addict as well as the family. This is what is happening in your case, Sanjiv."

Sanjiv couldn't respond; he just hung his head.

Pavitra added, "If he were a womanizer I could have divorced him easily. If he were an alcoholic or a drug addict, he would've destroyed only himself. But being a gambler, he is dragging all of us to an early grave. In fact, I just found out that when he went back to our country last month, he forged my signature and sold the house my parents left me. Would you believe he went through over sixty thousand dollars in one week?"

"Is this really true, Sanjiv? Did you really sink to that level? You actually committed crimes to support your habit—crimes against your own family," I replied, incredulous. I told him that I wanted him to hear what the Buddha said were the six evil consequences of gambling addiction:

As a winner he begets enmity;
As a loser he grieves over his loss;
There is actual loss of wealth in this very life;
His word is not relied upon;
He is despised by his friends and companions;

He is not sought after as a partner in marriage because
   people say, "He is a gambler; he cannot support a wife."[1]

Sanjiv asked almost belligerently, "So, Bhante, what do you suggest I do to overcome my problem? Do you know the reason why I
took to gambling? My wife is always nagging me, and she wants to
control all my movements. I don't have any space of my own. On
many occasions I was tempted to run away from home. You will
laugh when I say this, but there was a time I even wanted to be a
monk just to get away from her."

I quickly replied. "That's a good idea, Sanjiv! Why don't you
come to the temple and I'll make you a monk. You'll soon be rid
of your gambling habit."

"I can't do that, Bhante, because I love my children."

"If you really loved your children, you wouldn't have stolen
their money!" Pavitra put in angrily.

"You see, Bhante," said Sanjiv. "Even in front of you her behavior is full of disrespect for me."

"Sanjiv, are you proud of your behavior? I must tell you what I
think, very directly—you have a pattern of compulsive gambling
that disrupts your life and undermines the security of your family; you have even resorted to unethical acts to obtain money for
gambling. At this point, it appears that you have reached the final,
most desperate phase of your addiction. If you continue, Sanjiv,
then you are surely doomed."

Sanjiv's expression reflected that of a beaten man.

"Do you know the story of King Yudhisthira from chapter
twelve of the Mahabharata?" I asked. Sanjiv shook his head. "This
king could not stop gambling until he lost everything—including
his own freedom. He lost his kingdom, and then even wagered
his brothers, the clothes on their backs, and finally his wife. It is
unbelievable but true.

"In more recent times, I am aware of an individual in Los Angeles who was a multimillionaire; he drove a Rolls Royce, lived in a mansion, and owned a big company. However, he eventually lost every penny due to his gambling obsession. He and his family were out on the street. I can actually tell you more 'riches to rags' stories than I care to remember. You must listen to me, Sanjiv, if you and your family are to survive."

Sanjiv looked up at me in despair, but he was listening.

"In the Majjhima Nikaya, the Buddha said that thoughts can be looked at as being of two types. First, there are thoughts that lead to pain, distress, or grief—for yourself, for others, or for both yourself and others. Second, there are thoughts that *do not* lead to pain, distress, or grief for yourself, or for others. Please hear this, Sanjiv: whatever you think about frequently and ponder upon greatly, those will be the thoughts and feelings the mind will lean toward and crave.

"The Buddha spoke about how, as a bodhisattva before he was enlightened, he used this classification of thoughts to purify his mind. He said, 'When a thought arose, I considered whether or not it led to my pain or to the pain of others, obstructed wisdom, caused difficulties, or lead away from Nibbana. If I saw that it did, it automatically subsided.'"[2]

"To be truthful, I haven't thought much about Nibbana, Bhante, but I'll be grateful if you could help me overcome my addiction to gambling," Sanjiv said with humility. It seemed a good sign that he was finally admitting his problem.

"Sanjiv, if you want to change, I can teach you how to get rid of those thoughts of gambling, but there is one condition."

"What is the condition, Bhante?" Sanjiv asked meekly.

"The condition is that you will have to practice and apply to your life what I teach you. Is that understood?"

"Yes, Bhante," replied Sanjiv. "I'll do my best."

"In order to remove your addiction, your harmful and unwanted thoughts of gambling must be completely eradicated. And how does one do this? The Buddha has given five methods to remove unwanted thoughts.[3]

"First of all, attention should be diverted from the unwanted thought and given to some other thought. For example, when a small child is playing with something dangerous, you get the child to stop by substituting a safe toy for the dangerous one.

"Second, examination of the danger in the unwholesome thoughts connected to desire, hate, and delusion will lead to their abandonment, and they will subside. For example, you could think about the bad consequences that can occur because of gambling—like not having money to even buy food for your children.

"Third, one should ignore the unwanted thought by not paying attention to it, just as a man with good eyesight who doesn't want to see something would close his eyes.

"Fourth, attention should be given to stopping the unwanted thought from forming in the first place.

"Fifth, one should use one's mental strength to let go of the unwanted thought—to not give in to the unwanted thought by getting involved."

Sanjiv was still despondent. "Bhante," he said, "I'm not sure how to apply what you've just told me to overcome my weakness for gambling."

"Sanjiv, what I've just told you—in fact, what the Buddha just told you—can be applied to overcoming any weakness or addiction—not just gambling. You definitely possess all of the symptoms of a gambling addict. You also have problems coping with your feelings, and lying has become part of your lifestyle. You lie to your wife, to your children, to your friends, and most importantly to yourself. Everyone—including you—has lost confidence in you. Your financial problems have become increasingly overwhelming. You have become a deceitful and secretive person. You may be doing all this with the hope of hitting the jackpot, but instead you are dragging yourself deeper and deeper into debt.

"That being said, the first thing you must do, Sanjiv, is make up your mind that you want to change. Without doing this first, you will get nowhere. Tell yourself you must take control of your emotions. Repeat, 'I will not allow myself to be overpowered by the thought of gambling. I will not nourish that kind of thought. I will not feed that kind of thought. I will ignore that thought.' There is a movie called *A Beautiful Mind*, about the Nobel Prize winner Dr. John Nash, who was able to control his schizophrenia in exactly that way. I highly recommend that you watch the movie and learn from his story. You can apply what he did to your own life."

Gladly, I am happy to report that Sanjiv followed the Buddha's advice and eventually improved the quality of his thinking. He constantly made the effort to look the other way when unwanted thoughts about gambling entered his mind. He gradually learned how to reprogram his mind so he wouldn't feed the unwanted thoughts. He developed a thinking pattern that utilized strong thoughts (like his family's welfare) overcoming weak thoughts (like winning the jackpot at the local casino). He would visualize the strong overcoming the weak—and the weak thought would disappear.

As Sanjiv has demonstrated his willingness to overcome his addiction, he and Pavitra have become closer as a couple, both of them careful to exercise mutual respect. With the cessation of the gambling, their financial status has stabilized—and improves year by year.

> Whoso being heedless before,
> But is no more heedless,
> Illumines this world
> Like the moon freed from the clouds.[4]

◆ ◆ ◆ ◆ ◆ ◆

15 ◆ Dealing with Death

Jane had been a regular visitor to Dharma Vijaya Buddhist Vihara for about fifteen years. She was in her early fifties, married to a wonderful husband, and had no children. She dearly loved her two dogs and a cat, all three of whom had been with her for many years. Buster was a golden retriever with long shaggy ears; Princess, a white Pomeranian, was a spoiled dog that always got her way with "Mommy." Princess's haughtiness was exhibited even in her royal gait. Honey, the cat, was always playful.

Jane's love for these animals brought her much pleasure. She related a story about her cat, Honey, at our meditation class one evening when we had a discussion on compassion. Honey had never been neutered, and Jane was absolutely thrilled when Honey got pregnant. She assumed that the neighboring tomcat was the paramour. One day when she returned home from shopping she was amazed to see that the cat had delivered her litter of four kittens on Buster's dog bed. Buster usually didn't like anyone near his bed, but he had allowed Honey to use it as a maternity ward. Jane noticed that Buster was keeping a close eye on the newborns. Princess, as usual, was sprawled out on the floor in all her regal splendor; she seemed happy to welcome the new arrivals to their family. As Jane ended her story, she joked to the group: "I don't believe that old saying about 'fighting like cats and dogs.'"

I said, "Then we'll have to change that to 'living in harmony like cats and dogs.'"

It was Jane's custom to bring her pets to the temple to receive blessings whenever they got sick. Of course she immediately took them to the vet first for traditional treatment and medicine, but afterward she brought them to the temple for "that extra insurance." The animals were very well behaved, and they would sit quietly next to Jane while I chanted *pirith*. After I finished chanting I would tie the blessed string around their necks. I usually gave the pet holy water to drink, and to my surprise the sick pet would lap it up happily and look up at me as if saying, "I'm okay now."

Jane is a conscientious meditator who practices daily at home. She says that her pets join her and that they don't move until she finishes saying the loving-kindness meditation at the end. Her life is centered around her pets—so much so that on several occasions her husband Joe has complained that his wife neglects him.

One day Jane telephoned me in a panic. "Bhante, my son is no more. I don't want to live. Help me, Bhante, help me." She was crying and sobbing uncontrollably.

"Jane, calm down and tell me what happened."

"Bhante, my Buster died."

"How?" I asked.

"I went for my morning walk with Buster and Princess. I was holding the leash when suddenly Buster bolted and took off after another dog. He ran across the street just as a car turned the corner. It hit him full force and threw him against the curb. I ran to him, screaming his name. For just a second he looked up at me as if to say goodbye, then he closed his eyes and died right there in the street. Bhante, I can't believe it. What am I going to do without him?"

"Jane, I am so sorry. I will see you shortly. Don't panic, we are here for you."

That evening I went with one of my assistant monks to see her. She was completely lost in despair, and couldn't stop sobbing. Meanwhile, she clung to Princess, not letting her out of her arms.

I tried to console her by saying that in the ten years Buster was with her, she gave him all the comforts he could possibly want. I said that she had protected him and was as devoted to him as if he were her own son.

"I'm sure Buster was very grateful to you, Jane. He will probably be born again as someone very close to you," I said, trying to comfort her.

But she couldn't stop crying for Buster. "I will miss him every minute. I just can't live without him," she vowed sorrowfully.

"Jane, please try to get over your sadness and take care of your husband and your other pets. They need you. It is true that we feel sad when someone close to us passes away, but we have to remember that nothing is permanent in this world—including the pets we love.

"Please remember what the Buddha said, 'Here in this world, life is not predictable nor is it certain. Here, life is short with difficulties and suffering. Being born one then dies, without exception; whether from old age or another cause. All living beings meet Death!'[1]

"What we can do now is give merit to Buster," I continued. "We will arrange a memorial service at the temple tomorrow. Please come with your husband at five p.m."

"Bhante, what should I bring?" she asked.

"You can bring a picture of Buster, and some flowers to offer to the Buddha."

The next day Jane arrived with her husband and a few friends. We took them to the shrine hall, and I asked her to place the photograph of Buster on the altar. She refused; instead she kept the photograph close to her heart while crying nonstop.

"Bhante, please do something to bring Buster back to me. I can't believe he's dead."

This was a good opportunity to tell her the story of Kisa Gotami.

"During the time of the Buddha," I said, "there was a rich lady named Kisa Gotami. When her firstborn son suddenly died, she was so stricken with grief that she couldn't accept it. She went from house to house carrying the dead body of the five-month-old baby, asking for medicine to revive him.

"After a while the people in the street started laughing at her, and she couldn't understand their cruel reaction. Then an old man advised her, 'There is a good physician, a miracle maker staying in the city of Savatthi. He is the Buddha. Go to him—I'm sure he can help you.'

"Kisa Gotami went to Savatthi to find the Buddha. She was given directions as to where he was staying, and she went to him. When she was before the Buddha, she put the dead child down at his feet and pleaded with him to revive her son.

"'Please, Lord Buddha, this is my firstborn son. I know you can work miracles. Please bring him back to me,' she cried.

"The Buddha replied in a loving, compassionate manner, 'My dear sister, I am able to do that for you, but first I need you to bring me some mustard seeds from a house where there have been no deaths in the family. If you do this I will bring your son back to life.'

"She said, 'Thank you, Lord Buddha. I will return right away with the mustard seeds you have asked for.' Then she picked up the dead child and ran out into the city.

"Kisa held her dead baby son closely to her bosom as she went from house to house. At each house she asked, 'Please can you give me some mustard seeds?' The householder would return with a parcel of seeds and hand them to her.

"She then would say, 'Have you ever had a death in your family?'

"Inevitably the householder would reply that a parent, child, grandmother, nephew, or some other relative had died in their house. Kisa would then give back the parcel of mustard seeds saying, 'Thank you, master, but I cannot use this, it must come from a house that has not known death.'

"Going from house to house and having this scene repeated over and over again, she finally understood that she would not be able to find a house where the family had not faced death. She also understood that whenever there is birth, death is inevitable. With this understanding she went back to the Buddha, still carrying her dead child.

"She approached the Buddha and said, 'Lord Buddha, I have learned the lesson you set out for me to learn. There is no house where there has been no death. Therefore, I was unable to bring you the mustard seed you requested. I now know that my child is dead, and nothing can be done for him. Please teach me how to overcome my grief and suffering.'[2]

"The Buddha replied, 'All conditioned things—including human beings—are impermanent. With birth there is death, with arising there is ceasing. How can there be birth without death? You are grieving over the loss of your son. It was an unexpected early death.'

"Kisa Gotami learned her lesson about the impermanence of life. She felt that her grief and suffering had been lessened by the Buddha's words. She picked up her dead child and took it home to prepare it for cremation. It is stated that later she attained enlightenment."

After telling the story of Kisa Gotami, I talked more about the Buddha's teachings. "Jane," I said, "Buddhism helps us to understand the mystery of life. It is by understanding death that we understand life. Life and death are two ends of the same thread.

"On another occasion the Buddha explained that death can occur like the extinguishing of the light of an oil lamp, which can happen in one of four ways. He uses this oil lamp analogy to explain death in terms of four different types of karmic energy.

"*Ayukkaya* is when the body dies of natural causes in old age. This is like when all the oil in the lamp is used up but the wick is still remaining. *Kammakkaya* is when the body is not old, but the 'previous life' karma is finished and there is no more karmic energy for this life. This is like when the wick of the lamp has been burned up but there is still oil remaining. *Ubhayakkaya* is when the body dies of old age—and the karmic energy is finished. This is like when both the oil and the wick are used up. It describes the death of an enlightened being, or *arahat,* one who does not need to take another birth. *Upacchedaka* is when the body is neither old nor the karmic energy used up but when an outside force— such as an accident, tsunami, a terrorist act, or a driveby shooting occurs and life ends suddenly. This is like a gust of wind blowing out the flame of the lamp even though the oil and wick are still remaining.[3]

"According to the Buddha, there are two types of death. The first is the physical death that every human being is destined for from birth. The second is death in the minds and hearts of people. This second death is the reason for the Buddha's encouragement of all human beings to do good deeds for their families and society. If they do so, they will be remembered for what they have done after their deaths. If good deeds are not done while one is alive, then the person who dies in the flesh will also die in the hearts and minds of loved ones.

"Jane, I know it is very difficult for us as human beings to bear the loss of a loved one. However, we cannot waste our lives grieving for them. Do not forget that you have your husband and Princess and Honey, who still love and need you. Death does leave a scar that cannot be erased when we are very close to the departed one. I'm not telling you to forget Buster, but you must get on with your life. Keep the happy memories of your pet, but also remember that nothing in physical form is forever."

Jane was finally able to place Buster's picture on the altar. We conducted the memorial service and Jane went home with a lighter heart.

Where can one hide from death?
In the sky? No.
In the oceans? No.
In the mountains? No.
Nowhere can one hide from death.[4]

◆ ◆ ◆ ◆ ◆ ◆

16 ◆ Music and Chanting in Buddhism

In America I've been asked many times why there is no music in Buddhism. Each time I answer that this is a total misconception. Like all religions and cultures in the world, music and art has been closely associated with Buddhism—as it has with Hinduism, Judaism, Christianity, and Islam.

All of the world's major religions use chanting and prayers as part of their ritual and practice. In each case, these chants and prayers evolved into liturgical music—much of which was used to access the mystical experience for the performer, listener, or both. Music is calming and uplifting, while religion purifies the mind, and the combination of both encourages and inspires the listener to go within and seek peace and contentment.

The music found in the three branches of Buddhism—Theravada, Mahayana, and Vajrayana—all share the same origin. In each case music was used to aid meditation, enabling the mind to concentrate and become focused. All three branches developed chants with which to pass on their oral spiritual traditions and lineages. The chants all have their origin in the Sanskrit language, which was the language of scholars in ancient India. The Buddha's teaching is also recorded in Pali, the other ancient language of India. Theravada chanting is in Pali, while Mahayana and Vajrayana chanting is a combination of Sanskrit and the national language where the chant was transmitted. For example, when Japanese Buddhists chant the *okyo* (Mahayana Buddhist sutras), you will hear a combination of Sanskrit with the Japanese language.

The chanting in each of the three Buddhist traditions is musical, in that each uses tonal variation in the recitation and each uses "vocals" in the delivery. Theravada chants do not use instrumental accompaniment of any kind. Mahayana and Vajrayana chants utilize drums, gongs, conch shells and bells during the chanting.

In Theravada countries such as Sri Lanka, Thailand, Myanmar, Cambodia, and Laos, chanting is done by Buddhist monks using different melodies. Like the Gregorian chants of the Catholic Church in the Middle Ages, Buddhist chanting is usually intoned by monks in the context of rituals.

In Mahayana countries—China, Vietnam, Korea, and Japan—Buddhist rituals and their accompanying music can be quite elaborate.

In Vajrayana, the Tibetan branch of practice, music is a part of their chanting. They blow the conch shell, turn the musical prayer wheel, and keep time to the beat of the prayer bowl and drum. They even incorporate colorful ethnic costumes, masks, and dancing to further tell the story expressed in the music. Tibetan monks have perfected an amazing ability to chant in chords, which makes their chants sound magical and otherworldly.

In Sri Lanka, where most of the Buddhist chants were written, chanting was and continues to be performed primarily by Buddhist monks. Many of the chants are actual suttas, the sermons of the Buddha, which were converted to chants in order to preserve the messages in an oral tradition. The early recorders of the suttas converted them to verses with rhythm and meter, which made them easier to remember and transmit from generation to generation.

In fifteenth-century Sri Lanka there were three monks who wrote poetry, which they chanted to melodies of their own composition. These monks were Venerable Thotagamuwe Rahula Maha Thera, the author of *Kavyasekera* and *Salalihini Sandesaya*; Venerable Weedagama Maha Thera, the author of *Buduguna Alan-*

karaya and *Lovadasagara*; and Venerable Wettave Maha Thera, the author of *Guttilakavya*.

A Tibetan monk named Venerable Mahinda migrated to Sri Lanka from the Himalayan state of Sikkim in the early twentieth century and stayed for over four decades. During the period of the Sri Lankan struggle for independence (from the 1930s until 1948), he made a tremendous contribution to awaken the spirit of the people, writing patriotic songs that often called for the people to pursue freedom from the British. Mahinda said that his Dhamma was his songs. When he passed away in 1951 full honors were given to him by the Sri Lanka national government.

In more recent times, several Sri Lankan Buddhist monks have composed Buddhist songs. Venerable Rambukana Siddhartha, Venerable Pallegama Hemaratana, and Venerable Elle Gunawansa are among the most popular of these composers, whose songs speak of the Buddha's great qualities, social justice, and nationalism.

Most Sri Lankan Buddhist musical performers and composers have close associations with Buddhist temples. Many of them learned the teachings of the Buddha from Sangha members in their early years and have dedicated their lives to sharing the Dhamma through music.

During my thirty years in the United States, I have been invited to attend many Sri Lankan musical performances in this country, but I have always been reluctant to go. I know that some of the members of the Sri Lankan community have very conservative mental conditioning and they might object to my presence. Their view is that monks should not attend musical performances. Nevertheless, because of my personal friendship with the Sri Lankan singer and composer Dayaratna Ranatunga, I attended one of his performances about seven years ago. He welcomed me and the other Sangha members in my group warmly, and we enjoyed the Buddhist songs performed by him and his wife, Amara.

A year after we enjoyed this pleasant concert experience, Sunil Edirisinghe, another popular singer, arrived in Los Angeles. I had met him previously at the Forest Hermitage in Kanduboda, Sri Lanka, so I presumed he was a good Buddhist practitioner and therefore decided to attend his concert. When we arrived we were escorted to our seats and felt quite at ease. However, to my complete amazement, the announcer's sarcastic opening words to the audience were, "Ha ha, even Buddhist monks are present here. I don't understand why."

We suddenly felt quite uneasy. The announcer's unfortunate and inappropriate remarks caused a stir, and heads turned in our direction. We stayed for a while, but after a few songs I thought it was best to quietly leave the hall.

Believe it or not, this small incident caused quite a controversy in our Sri Lankan community. There was considerable discussion at private gatherings about whether monks should attend musical performances or whether concertgoing was against the Vinaya. Some conservative and ill-informed folks spoke against me and the other Sangha members for attending. Others felt that our attendance at the performance was perfectly acceptable. Some of the community members came to the Dharma Vijaya temple to formally discuss what for them had become an issue.

Keerthi was the first to open the discussion. "Bhante, I grew up in Kandy, where all my life I heard the beating of the drums—morning and evening—coming from the main temple. The drums are played before the monks begin chanting as an offering to the Buddha. Whether it is in Sri Lanka or here in Los Angeles, when the monks chant, it is music to my ears. I do not see anything wrong in monks attending musical performances," he said.

Channa was quick to respond, quoting in Pali number seven from the Eight Precepts: "*Naccagitaraditharisukadassanamala gandhavilepanadharanamandana vibhusanatthana veramani sikkhapadam samadhiyama.*"

I responded, "Channa, thank you for reminding me of the Eight Precepts. What you have quoted is indeed something that laypeople observe—mostly on full moon days. It may apply to Buddhist monks, too. But do you know what it means?"

He replied, "It means, 'I undertake the training rule to abstain from dancing, singing, music shows, wearing garlands, using perfumes, and beautifying with cosmetics.'"

"Channa, the precept you just quoted is for laypeople to use to discipline themselves during a retreat," I said in return. "Originally the seventh of the Eight Precepts said '*Malam na dhare na ca gandamacare*,' which means that one should not wear ornaments nor use perfumes. There was no prohibition against music. This is found in one of the oldest collection of suttas, Sutta Nipata: Dhammika Sutta."

Channa said, "Why is it that the precept now excludes music?"

"Channa, there is a sutta in the Anguttara Nikaya where the Buddha mentions that during the observance of *uposatha* (full moon days) if someone follows the example of the *arahat* in these eight ways for that day and night that it would be very fruitful, very beneficial for them. These are times when the people have the opportunity to quiet and develop their minds, so of course music would be inappropriate then."

"Okay, Bhante, I can see why a change might have been made. Otherwise when the people gathered for the observance of the full moon days, they might have music and turn it into a party," Keerthi said.

"Let me tell you the story of Sona, an energetic monk who lived during the Buddha's time," I continued. "Sona meditated all day and night, but could not develop his concentration. He finally decided to give up his robe and return to his former life as a layman. The Buddha appeared before him before he disrobed and said, 'How is your meditation coming, Sona?'

"'I have been following the technique you taught us, Lord, but

I'm not getting anywhere,' said Sona. 'I sit so much in meditation that my legs are turning green. I don't mind the pain, but I can't seem to concentrate. I'm giving up and returning to the world.'

"The Buddha replied, 'I heard you were a well-known lute player before you became a monk. Is this true?'

"'Yes, that is true, Lord.'

"'Tell me, when the strings were too tight on your lute, was the sound melodious and pleasant?' asked the Buddha.

"'No, my Lord,' replied Sona. 'The sound was tense and shrill.'

"'When the strings were too loose, was the lute melodious and playable?'

"'No, Lord. The sound was irritating and off-key.'

"The Buddha then asked, 'When the strings were neither too tight nor too loose, was the lute melodious and playable?'

"'Yes, Lord, when the strings are properly balanced, the music is sweet and melodious,' replied Sona.

"Then the Buddha explained, 'It is the same with our effort. When it is either too eager or too lax, the result of our effort will be lacking. But if we are to follow the Middle Path and develop balance in our practice, the result of our effort will be satisfactory. Furthermore, we should practice the Middle Path as our overriding guide in all of our everyday activities, using mindfulness to observe our thoughts and feelings.'[1]

"You can see that the Buddha was aware of music and its use as a tool to explain the Dhamma," I remarked.

Channa said, "Of course, before becoming the Buddha, Prince Siddhartha studied and played music. It doesn't mean that he approved of it. Is there any sutta that says the Buddha approved of music?"

"Yes, Channa. The Sakkapanna Sutta[2] tells the story.

"One day when the Buddha was in deep meditation, Sakka, the lord of the gods, decided to pay him a visit. He was accompanied by his musician, Pancasikha, who offered to distract the

Buddha's attention from his profound state of *samadhi* on the condition that he be allowed to marry Suriyaraccasa, his sweetheart. Sakka agreed, and Pancasikha said, 'I will get his attention.' He played his lute while singing a song extolling the Buddha, the Dhamma, the *arahats*, and love." I repeated some of the verses from the song:

> To one sweating, the breeze is a joy,
> Like a cool drink for the thirsty.
> Your glowing beauty is precious to me,
> As the Dhamma is to *arahats*.
>
> In the summer heat, the elephant seeks
> A lotus pool with petals floating.
> I seek in you the same salvation.
>
> As the Sakyan son in deep meditation
> Determined to achieve the goal,
> Intent I am to receive your love.
>
> As the Sage enjoys enlightenment attained,
> So will I, when joined with you.
>
> If Sakka were to grant me a wish
> I'd wish for you, it's you I desire.

"When he heard this, the Buddha said, 'Pancasikha, the sound of your strings blends so well with your song, and your song with the strings, that neither prevails excessively over the other. When did you compose those verses on the Buddha, the Dhamma, the *arahats*, and love?'

"The very fact that this early sutta included the actual verses of a song that praised the Buddha, the Dhamma, the *arahats*, and love—all at the same time—is proof that the Buddha admired and approved of the art of music. This last comment by the Buddha is actually a critique of the song, so that Buddha was the first Buddhist music critic. It also shows the Buddha's knowledge of music and the instruments that are played to produce it. He knew about tuning the lute to make sure it was balanced and perfect. In no way did he show any displeasure in even the lyrics of this sutta, which expressed the singer's profound love for his lady.

"The Buddha didn't discourage or condemn Pancasikha for his feelings and desires. Therefore, to try to make the Buddha appear to be so far removed from us is incorrect. The Buddha was such an effective spiritual teacher and guide due to his clear understanding of the realities of human emotions. The Buddha knew and loved and appreciated everything human—including love, music, and all of the arts."

When I finished speaking, Keerthi responded, "Bhante, if the Buddha did, in fact, appreciate music, then I think we should consider writing melodies for our suttas and using them as another tool to share Buddhism with the world."

"Keerthi, I think you have a very good idea. It reminds me of a story from the first century B.C.E., when the Indian emperor Kanishka, whose grandfather was Chinese, had a strong desire to spread Buddhism in China. After deep contemplation he thought that the easiest way to introduce Buddhism to China was through the visual arts and music.

"He commissioned many sculptors in India to create Buddha statues. They all refused, however, fearing that they could not do justice to the Buddha's sublime and serene form. Alexander the Great had established a connection between Greece and India, so the emperor was quite familiar with Greek sculpture. He asked the Greek artists for help in creating a statue of the Buddha. The sculptors had no idea about the Buddha and his teaching, so it is probable that they used their image of Apollo, the Greek sun god, as the model for the first Buddha statue. This became what is now known as the Gandhara style of Buddhist art.

"At the same time that the emperor was seeking to have the Buddha's image portrayed in sculpture, he encouraged the Buddhist monks to create a stage play about the life of Sariputra and Moggallana, the Buddha's foremost disciples. What resulted from this request was the creation entitled *Sariputtaprakarana*. The stage play and the first Greek Buddha statues were sent to China as part of a royal Indian goodwill mission. The emperor also sent monks on this goodwill mission, and they were the first Buddhist missionaries to China.

"As a result of this first mission, and subsequent missions, the Chinese quickly embraced Buddhism. Later it was introduced to Korea and Japan. It wasn't long before these countries accepted Buddhism as their primary religion, and it fused with their culture through music and art."

Channa was still skeptical. "Bhante, the main goal for a Buddhist is to attain Nibbana. If our mind goes toward music, will that not be a hindrance to our goal?"

I knew very well how Channa's mind was working, so I said, "What you just said reminds me of an ancient legend from Sri Lanka.

"In a country village the women were harvesting rice and singing their traditional songs about unity, friendship, and *anicca*, or impermanence. The sixty monks who had been listening intently to the women's songs suddenly attained *arahat*hood.

"Music can be a spark for making Buddhist concepts real, Channa. The sound made by an instrument, such as a drum, a bell, or a lute, can become a symbol for the concept of *anatta*, or no-self. In meditation, for example, if we listen to the bell when it is struck, our mind can follow it until it fades away. The first strong sound eventually dissolves into nothingness—much in the same way that we as humans appear on the earth and eventually pass away.

"Music can also affect perceptions and emotions, and can even alter mental states. Therefore, music can act as a conduit between the phenomenal and the sacred worlds. I believe that chanting and other kinds of ritual music can bring us to an altered state of consciousness. In that state we come into contact with high vibrational states of reality, the spiritual abodes of peace, harmony, and oneness. If we use music as an accompaniment to visualizing loving-kindness, then our meditation can be used for the enlightenment of the whole world."

> Silence alone leads not to Wisdom;
> But with the cultivation of awareness;
> Seeing the world as it truly is and thus
> Choosing goodness is wisdom gained.[3]

◆ ◆ ◆ ◆ ◆ ◆

17 ◆ The Bhikkhuni Order

The Buddha established the orders of *bhikkhu* (monks) and *bhikkhuni* (nuns), giving equal rights to both males and females. In 232 B.C.E. Buddhism was introduced to Sri Lanka by the son of the Indian emperor Asoka, Arahat Mahinda, who established the bhikkhu order there. Arahat Mahinda's sister, Arahat Sanghamitta, came at his invitation, enabling the establishment of the bhikkhuni order in Sri Lanka. Both the bhikkhu and bhikkhuni orders thrived in the country until 1017 C.E., when there were no bhikkhunis and only a few thousand bhikkhus left. This was due to many reasons: war, drought, and famine that raged throughout the country. It was possible to strengthen the bhikkhu order with help from Burma and Thailand, but there were no bhikkhunis in either of these countries and the bhikkhuni order could not be reestablished.

In the late 1970s Master Hsing Yun of the Fo Kuang Shan temple in Taiwan began to realize his vision of establishing Buddhist temples in America. Fo Kuang Shan is one of the major Mahayana "Pure Land" temples in the world. The first temple Master Hsing Yun founded in America was originally located in Gardena, California, but it eventually evolved into what is now the magnificent Hsi Lai temple in Hacienda Heights, southeast of Los Angeles. The Gardena temple, as well as the Hsi Lai temple, was originally developed and managed by Buddhist nuns who were sent here from Taiwan. The nuns' devotion, dedication, and energy were truly inspiring, and I was greatly impressed. At the time, I did whatever I could do to help them establish their temple and get it running.

Seeing the devotion of these dedicated nuns made me realize that one of my life goals would be to reestablish the bhikkhuni order in the Theravada tradition. Since the devotion and dedication of these nuns is unparalleled anywhere in the Buddhist world, I decided that I would visit their headquarters in Taiwan. I wanted to explore the idea of having the Chinese nuns help reestablish the Sri Lankan Theravada bhikkhuni order. In October 1997, I was in communication with Master Hsing Yun, who invited me to Fo Kuang Shan in the Taiwanese city of Kao-hsiung.

When I visited the Taiwanese temple, I witnessed the practice of the nuns, which began at 3:30 a.m. when they joined the monks for chanting and two hours of meditation. The nuns worked tirelessly in the gardens and fields, pruning trees, weeding, planting, and harvesting vegetables. They also performed many other temple-related chores throughout the day. I couldn't help but notice the respect the nuns had not only for their fellow bhikkhunis but for the male Sangha members as well. It was remarkable how well they worked with one another in mutual cooperation. When it came to ceremony and ritual matters, however, the nuns always respectfully deferred to the monks. There were no signs of competition or animosity whatsoever.

While I was visiting the temple in Taiwan I was reminded that in the fifth century c.e., Devasara, a Sri Lankan bhikkhuni, went to China with five nuns and established a bhikkhuni order. This order is mentioned in the Chinese chronicles and is also discussed in *Buddhist Texts through the Ages*, published in 1954 by the Buddhist scholar Edward Conze. The bhikkhuni lineage established by Devasara exists to this day, not only in Chinese Buddhism but also in Korean and Vietnamese Buddhism.

I believed that we could reestablish the Theravada bhikkhuni order in Sri Lanka if we had the help of the Chinese monks and nuns as well as the support of the Sri Lankan Sangha members. I knew that I would face an almost insurmountable wall of opposition from the Sangha members in Thailand, Burma, Cambodia, Laos, and parts of Sri Lanka. I also expected to encounter opposition from various conservative Buddhist groups around the world.

My next step was to write a letter to Master Hsing Yun requesting that he invite a few *dasa sil matas* from Sri Lanka and train them for full ordination. *Dasa sil matas* translates as "Ten Precept mothers"—these are women who take the same Ten Precents as *samaneras*, or novice monks, but are not recognized by the Sangha as having any status or place in our Buddhist hierarchy. In Sri Lanka they wear yellow clothing and reside in their own nunneries. In Thailand and Laos these women wear white clothing, shave their heads, and are called *maechi*. They provide a variety of services—mostly childcare for orphans, counseling, and social service work. There are similar groups in Myanmar, where they are known as *silashin*, and in Cambodia, where they are called *donjee*.

I discussed my vision for reviving the ordination of bhikkhunis in Sri Lanka with our resident senior adviser at my temple in Los Angeles, the late Venerable Dr. Havanpola Ratanasara, who approved of the plans, which began with the goal of ordaining a woman at my temple, Dharma Vijaya, in Los Angeles. His wisdom and insight helped us to overcome many obstacles in regard to the ordination of nuns. Venerable Pannila Ananda, the secretary of Dharma Vijaya, also approved of my idea, and after many consultations with senior monks living in the United States, the three of us decided to begin our work.

However, Venerable Dr. Ellawela Nandissara, who was living in Dharma Vijaya at the time, vehemently objected to the idea of ordaining a woman at our temple. There were many arguments and discussions with Venerable Nandissara, who never gave us his approval.

"In order to have bhikkhunis, you must have practicing bhikkhunis. Venerable Piyananda, you have no practicing bhikkhunis," he said firmly.

I answered by saying, "During the time of the Buddha, the first bhikkhuni ordination took place in the fifth year after the Buddha's enlightenment.[1] Although women were not considered equal to men at that time, the Buddha allowed women to enter the order. The Buddha's words were 'I allow nuns to be ordained by monks.'"[2]

Venerable Nandissara countered, "It is true. The Buddha gave ordination to women at the request of his stepmother, Mahapajapati, but he specifically stated that Eight Important Rules must be adopted and followed. Arahat Sanghamitta, the daughter of Emperor Asoka of India, established the order of nuns in Sri Lanka but it disappeared by the twelfth century. There are no Theravada bhikkhunis anywhere, so how can you establish the order?"

I was prepared for his objection. "When the first bhikkhunis were ordained, the Buddha said unequivocally that monks can give ordination to nuns. In his second statement, which I call an amendment to the first statement, he said that both monks and nuns must be present during the initiation ceremonies for nuns." I then asked Venerable Nandissara, "How much time elapsed between the Buddha's first statement and the second statement? Why do you think the Buddha made the second statement?"

He replied, "It is very difficult to answer your first question, Venerable Piyananda, because Buddhist history doesn't give us an exact length of time that went by between the first and second statements. However, in regard to your second question, do you not remember the *atta garudhamma*, or the Eight Important Rules the Buddha gave before he allowed the ordination of his stepmother, Mahapajapati?"[3]

"Yes, Venerable Nandissara, I remember very well," I replied.

He continued, "The Buddha required both monks and nuns to be present at bhikkhuni ordinations because, according to the sixth, which you had quoted, a novice bhikkhuni must train with an ordained bhikkhuni for two years before she can take her higher ordination."

I responded, "Venerable sir, I think the Eight Important Rules you are referring to were not actually given by the Buddha himself. The sixth of the eight rules is unbelievable because, since Mahapajapati was the first nun to be ordained, there were no other nuns in existence. In our case, after we ordain the first Theravada nuns, we will allow those first to train the subsequent candidates. You have to start somewhere.

"Furthermore, the first rule of the Eight Important Rules you are referring to makes no sense whatsoever. It states that a senior nun, even with a hundred years of higher ordination, should worship and pay obeisance to a young monk who has only obtained higher ordination on that very day. Do you think the Buddha, with all of his intelligence and wisdom, and his record of treating males and females equally, would ever say such a thing? Haven't you noticed the change of Pali language used in the *garudhamma*? It is in a later style, which leads me and many other scholars to believe that the Eight Important Rules were added later by the Sangha after the Buddha's time. Some of the monks in those days most probably came from Brahmin families where there was no equality between men and women."

Venerable Nandissara got angry with me and said, "Venerable Piyananda, you don't have *saddha*, or faith. You even doubt the Tripitaka. Why should I talk to you any more?" At this point he rose to leave, but I respectfully asked him to remain seated.

"Venerable sir," I humbly said, "the female candidates who will come to us for ordination seek nothing from us. Their only desire is to observe the precepts so they can develop themselves spiritually and follow the same path we do as monks."

Venerable Nandissara continued, "Furthermore, during the ordination ceremony there are so many questions that the novices are asked by the preceptor. Among them are twenty-four questions that would be embarrassing for a man to ask a woman. That's another reason why a nun is needed at a bhikkhuni's ordination ceremony."

"Venerable sir," I replied, "after the ordination of Mahapajapati, nuns were ordained for over fifteen years without any problems. The Buddha may have made his second statement about having both monks and nuns present at the bhikkhuni ordination because of those delicate questions you are referring to. Yet, he did not cancel the first statement about allowing monks to ordain nuns in the first place. That's why I'm saying that the second statement was most likely an amendment to the first—much the same way that we have amendments to our constitution here in America." We argued further, but neither side gave in.

Nevertheless, in spite of Venerable Nandissara's objections we decided to give a novice's ordination to a Thai woman, Chutima Vucharatawintra, who was a suitable candidate. We informed all of the Sri Lankan monks in the United States of our decision, and on May 23, 1988, Chutima's *samaneri* ordination ceremony was conducted at my temple. The abbot of Wat Thai and several other Thai monks came to show their support.

In the years that immediately followed, Venerable Nandissara's opposition to the ordination was supported by a small conservative faction of the Sri Lankan community, but the majority of American-based Sri Lankan monks, as well as several high-ranking monks in Sri Lanka, continued their efforts to reestablish the bhikkhuni order.

In 1995, a symposium was held in Southern California by a Buddhist women's group and was attended by approximately 150 people, including several men. The main objective of this meeting was to gain support for the bhikkhuni order. Many active Western feminists showed up who passionately vented their feelings. I thought their behavior was most unbecoming for Buddhist practitioners.

A European woman mentioned the name of a leading senior monk in Sri Lanka who was openly opposed to the bhikkhuni order. She stated that if he were present in the audience she would "slipper" him. This is an insulting term in most of Asia—it means taking off your rubber slipper and hitting the other person in the face with it.

The deputy abbot of Wat Thai, Venerable Samahitho, was seated beside me with his assistant. They wanted to leave at once. I dissuaded them from leaving right away, and asked them to stay until I delivered my talk.

The symposium moderator announced my speech, and I went to the podium. I began by saying, "I understand the anger and frustration that is being displayed here today. However, since we are Buddhists, we must learn to overcome these feelings. If we cross the red line of anger, there is no way that we can achieve our goal.

"As you know, as Buddhists we believe in rebirth. I strongly believe, therefore, that Buddhist monks who object to the bhikkhuni order are to be reborn in Thailand as women. In Thailand it is very difficult to be given the bhikkhuni ordination; therefore, we shouldn't get angry with the monks who object, but offer them sympathy instead. Should they decide to become a bhikkhuni in their life as a Thai female, they most certainly will be denied.

"In the same manner, those who speak vindictively against the Sangha will undoubtedly be born as dogs in Sri Lanka and Thailand. I promise you! When monks go *pindapata*, making the morning alms collection, in Sri Lanka and Thailand, some dogs are in the habit of attacking them. I see this as a continuation of the actions of a previous birth. I hope that at least a few of you will understand my humor."

After the meeting Venerable Samahitho congratulated me on my speech and said that he was glad he stayed. The symposium's attendees completely understood my message and subsequently toned down their attitudes considerably.

In May 1996 the late Venerable Dr. Mapalagama Wipulasara Maha Thera, at that time the general secretary of the Maha Bodhi Society in India, organized a full bhikkhuni ordination ceremony for Theravada aspirants. He interviewed hundreds of potential candidates in Sri Lanka and selected ten women who were already *dasa sil matas*. He performed the first ordination ceremony for these women in Sri Lanka and made them *samaneri*. Later, he took these ten novices with him to Sarnath and gave them full ordination. I was happy to have participated in that ceremony, and with the following text I would like to share with you a section of my talk that was delivered at the Sarnath ordination:

Arahat Sanghamitta provided an immense legacy of social service to the people of Sri Lanka when she established the bhikkhuni order there.

On the ancient stone pillar at Mihintale in Sri Lanka it says that during the first century B.C.E., Buddhist nuns were the first group to establish health clinics for the benefit of the poor and the sick.

According to the Buddha's teachings, every human being has the right to follow the religious path if it is his or her wish. I feel that this ordination today marks a great opportunity to correct the situation where females had been refused permission to join the bhikkhuni order for over a thousand years.

We are gathered here today to restore the full opportunity to anyone who wishes to participate in Buddhist monastic life. Becoming a member of the Sangha is a commitment to follow the Vinaya, the monastic rules of discipline. To quote the Buddha, "The monk, nun, male or female lay-disciple who practices fully according to the Teaching, who is endowed with correctness in the practice of the Teaching, and who lives in perfect conformity with righteousness and truth, can be deemed to honor, esteem, venerate, revere and worship the Buddha in the highest degree."[4]

We must always remember that the key to our Buddhist practice is the elimination of ego. While that is a long-term project, as Sangha members we can help ourselves and others by developing and practicing humility.

While the path of monastic life is not an easy one, the steps and the structure have been kindly given to us by the Buddha, in the form of the Vinaya. In these times of change, for a variety of reasons traditionalists will undoubtedly continue to be opposed to the ordination of bhikkhunis. It is inevitable that politics and special agenda items play a part on both sides of the argument. For this very reason, it is most important that we monks adhere to the Vinaya, so we can gain the confidence and trust of those opposed to the reestablishment of the bhikkhuni order.

By the same token, we cannot blame any of the Sangha members for being fearful of women of the extreme feminist elements who ask for ordination. Oftentimes these women come with political and social agendas that oppose certain aspects of the Vinaya. This creates disunity in the Sangha, rather than unity, and as the Buddha said, "*Sukkha Sanghassa sammagi*,"—unity is the great happiness among the Sangha.[5]

We sincerely believe that the reestablishment of the bhikkhuni order is essential to the fulfillment of the Buddha's vision. By overcoming the obstacles to the ordination of nuns, we have given equal opportunity to everyone to spend their lives in the service of the Sangha and in pursuing the Buddha's path to enlightenment.

As a longtime supporter of the campaign to reestablish the bhikkhuni order, I would ask these pioneers not to let themselves get involved in political disputes, nor give in to criticism. I would ask you instead to bear any difficulties you encounter with humility, and in the spirit of the Vinaya.

As the Buddha said in the Brahmajala Sutta,

"Monks, if outsiders should speak against me, against my teaching, or against my disciples, you should not be angry, or hold that against them. If you were angry with them, how would you know if they were right or wrong?

"Also, if outsiders should praise me, my teachings, or my disciples, you should not be pleased or proud. If you were pleased or proud, how would you know if they were over-praising us?

"Therefore, whether people speak for or against me, my teaching, or my disciples, be neither proud nor angry. Rather, be impartial, and acknowledge it if they are right, or calmly explain where they are wrong. Furthermore, both anger and pride would be against your own spiritual development."[6]

Many success stories in regard to the ordination of Theravada Buddhist nuns have taken place since our first one here in America. In West Virginia, at the Bhavana Society, Venerable Dr. Henepola Gunaratana began ordaining bhikkhunis soon after we began the practice in Los Angeles. In Sri Lanka two organizations currently prepare women for the bhikkhuni ordination. One of them was established by the late Venerable Talalle Dhammaloka Anunayake Maha Thera. The other one was founded by the Venerable Inamaluwe Sumanangala Nayake Maha Thera, abbot of the magnificent cave temple known as the Golden Temple of Dambulla.

When there were no Theravada bhikkuni ordinations, a Sri Lankan woman named Nitha Gunaratne, who was formerly a schoolteacher, became a Zen Buddhist nun. Recently she received her higher ordination at the Golden Temple of Dambulla in Sri Lanka, and she now lives in Minneapolis, Minnesota, teaching Buddhism and meditation to her American students.

In 1999 at my temeple, a Thai woman named Prem Suksa-wat, who is a psychiatrist, was referred to me and became a *samaneri*. She later requested higher ordination as a bhikkhuni, and I arranged for her to go to Fo Kuang Shan temple in Taiwan for her ceremony. Venerable Dr. Gunaratana, Venerable Hinbunne Kondanna, and I participated in her ordination ceremony.

In 2002, a Burmese devotee of mine, a very fine woman doctor named Khin Swe Win, wanted to become a bhikkhuni. Venerable U Silananda, a well-known Burmese meditation teacher, personally requested that I perform her *samaneri* ordination and give her the name Gunasari. With the support of our good Thai friend Kung Pongsavas she later received full ordination in Sri Lanka, and now lives in Riverside, California, teaching her own devotees.

The gate is now open for any qualified candidate to enter the bhikkhuni order.

> One rid of defilements,
> Filled with virtues,
> Self-controlled and truthful
> Is worthy to wear the saffron robe.[7]

◆ ◆ ◆ ◆ ◆

18 ◆ Marriage Ceremonies

When I first came to the United States I quickly understood that I would have to adapt my Sri Lankan ways to my new environment if I wanted to thrive. This was particularly obvious to me during my first winter in Chicago. Sri Lanka is a tropical island where you rarely even need a sweater. Chicago has the "hawk," the icy cold wind that blows from the North—so I changed from wearing only my cotton robes and sandals to also wearing an overcoat and shoes with my traditional garb.

I also understood that our South Asian Theravada Buddhism would have to adapt to its new environment if it were to become a viable spiritual path for Americans. It had been my intention from the beginning to serve not only Sri Lankan Americans in the traditional ways of their home country, but to serve all Americans in what I hoped would become the newly evolved Buddhist ways in America.

I desired to share a Buddhist way of life, to share the practices that would support the personal development many Americans seemed to want. I also desired to have the Buddha's teachings thrive in this country, adapting to the host culture in such a way that new practices would be established that fit the American way of life.

In 1980, four years after my arrival here, I started the first of these new practices, which, I believe, was the performance of the first Theravada wedding ceremonies in the Western world. The senior monks of the temple decided that performing Buddhist wedding rites was not against the Vinaya rules.

The first fifteen wedding ceremonies were performed for American couples who greatly appreciated being able to have a ceremony that reflected their Buddhist perspective. In 2001 I was approached about performing a wedding ceremony for a Sinhalese couple, and this sixteenth ceremony was met with a bit of resistance from a few members of the Sri Lankan community.

Dr. Gamini Jayasinghe, a founding board member of the Dharma Vijaya temple, asked me if I would perform the wedding ceremony for his daughter, Amali. We were very happy to do this for Amali and her family, as we have known the young woman since she was a child attending our Sunday school.

The groom was Catholic and Father Flavian Wilathgamuwa, a close friend of mine, was invited to the wedding to give his blessing. When Venerable Pannila Ananda and I arrived at the Hilton Waterfront Beach Resort in Huntington Beach, we were welcomed in the lobby by a traditional Sri Lankan drummer who led us to the reception hall. He took us to the *poruwa* (traditional dais), where the couple stood for the ceremony. The couple welcomed us with the traditional offering, a sheaf of betel leaves.

We then proceeded to perform a brief Buddhist ceremony, which started when I tied the thumbs of the bride and groom together with a blessed thread. Then Venerable Ananda and I poured blessed water on the palms of their hands while we chanted the Maha Mangala Sutta. After this, wedding rings were exchanged along with the traditional Buddhist wedding vows. Father Flavian gave the couple a blessing, and the ceremony was concluded American style—the groom kissing the bride.

Immediately after the ceremony Venerable Ananda and I were escorted from the reception hall to our car. It is not appropriate for monks to attend the wedding reception in Sri Lankan culture.

I want to mention that this was a modified wedding ceremony, because in the Sri Lankan tradition they can be much longer and far more elaborate, depending on the bride's family, and the bridal couple's wishes.

The first wedding that the senior monks and I planned had the bride and groom entering the shrine room of the temple carrying lit candles of different colors. They approached the altar and lit the central candle together. This symbolized the oneness of their existence from that moment. Then the bride and the groom each lit one stick of different colored incense and placed them together on the altar. The smoke that emanated from the two sticks became one color as it rose and symbolized the fact that even though they were two different people, from that point forward they must live together as one in harmony.

The vows that we wrote for the couples to share were inspired by the words of the Buddha in the Sigalovada Sutta in Digha Nikaya:

[Name of groom], do you take [name of bride] to be your lawful wife, and agree to take on the responsibilities of a husband? Will you treat your wife with love and respect? Will you honor her and always speak gently? Will you be honest and faithful to her at all times? Will you share the authority, responsibilities, and duties of the household with her? Will you give her gifts with love and kindness?

[Name of bride], do you take [name of groom] to be your lawful husband and agree to take on the responsibilities of a wife? Will you treat your husband with love and respect? Will you honor him and always speak gently? Will you be honest and faithful to him at all times? Will you share the authority, responsibilities, and duties of the household with him? Will you give him gifts with love and kindness?

After the exchange of vows, we would pronounce the couple husband and wife, chant *paritta*, and give them our blessings.

A couple of days after Amali Jayasinghe and Reshan Cooray were married I received a few anonymous e-mails criticizing me for my involvement in the wedding. This created some division in the Sri Lankan society in Los Angeles. Some individuals suggested that I was initiating the eventual destruction of the Sangha. Some individuals, however, praised me for my initiative, while still others questioned me about the Vinaya and what it says about weddings.

One of the e-mails I received went like this:

> You have conducted a Buddhist wedding ceremony in a
> hotel. It is a shame for a Buddhist monk even to be seen
> at a wedding. Monks should discourage unions that pro-
> duce individuals to inhabit this world which is full of
> suffering. The Buddha said that monks should give up
> all pleasures, renounce everything, and work toward the
> ultimate goal of Nirvana. Don't destroy Buddhism. Don't
> introduce hippie religions. Return to Sri Lanka or give up
> your robes!

I myself was not offended by these messages, but some of the devotees at my temple took it upon themselves to reply to such harsh e-mails. One member replied to the anonymous e-mails using the following form letter, "It is a well-known fact that the Buddha was invited to homes to advise and bless new couples. Most probably, these were the first Buddhist marriage ceremonies."

This response on my behalf put him at the receiving end of a barrage of anonymous e-mails, many of them questioning his authority to give an answer and some of them going so far as to attack him personally.

Fortunately, an erudite Buddhist scholar, Dr. Ananda Guruge, explained to one and all in an e-mail response that there was nothing wrong with a Buddhist monk conducting a wedding ceremony. He proved and supported his statement by citing early Buddhist texts. This silenced the uninformed folks who had spoken out against me, and it expanded their knowledge of Buddhist teaching and traditions as well.

After this incident, Kumara and Rani, a married couple, came to ask me more about what Dr. Gururge had said. This gave me the opportunity to explain how the Buddha advised the lay community to live a successful and happy married life.

"There are four qualities that the Buddha said were important for a successful marriage," I told them. "These are: *saddha*, faith in your partner; *sila*, good conduct; *caga*, generosity; and *panna*, wisdom."[1]

Kumara said, "Bhante, I know the Pali words you just gave us, but can you tell us a little bit more about how they apply to a marriage?"

"Of course," I began. "*Saddha*, in this case, means that you will trust one another and that both of you will be honest with the other. *Sila*, in this instance, means that you will refrain from all forms of sexual misconduct. This means that you will never again even look at another man or woman with lust in your mind or heart. *Caga*, in regard to marriage, means sharing everything with each other and your families—not just your money or material possessions but also your time and love. And the most important quality, *panna*, for a husband and wife, means to do all you can to learn about each other and to have understanding."

Rani asked, "Bhante, does the husband have special duties to perform for the wife?"

"Yes, the Buddha gave his advice on this matter more than twenty-five centuries ago, and it is just as relevant today as it was then, because it is down-to-earth and practical. The Buddha advised husbands: First of all, honor your wife with kind and respectful words. Second, never insult her, or even slight her, even in jest. Third, be faithful to her. Fourth, once trust is established, give her your worldly goods to manage. And finally, don't forget to remember her with gifts and special treats—particularly on special days."[2]

Kumara said, "That's great for the wives, but what do we husbands get?"

"The husbands get a great deal, Kumara. First of all, even though it's difficult in today's frantic world, your wife should organize her work in such a way that she can provide a neat and orderly home for you. Second, she should be polite and generous to those who support her in her work. Third, she should always be faithful and true to you, just as you will be to her. Fourth, she will manage, maintain, and protect the family's material possessions. Finally, she will perform all her duties skillfully and diligently, both at home and outside."[3]

Rani smiled and said, "If we go by these rules we'll both make out okay in this arrangement."

I continued, "It is interesting to note some of the advice given by the parents of Visakha before her marriage. As we know, Visakha was one of the main supporters of the Buddha. Her father said, 'A wife should not criticize her husband and parents-in-law in front of other people. Neither should their weaknesses or household quarrels be reported elsewhere. A wife should not listen to the stories or reports of other households. This advice applies to both marriage partners.'"[4]

Kumara became excited upon hearing this advice and said, "Bhante, my wife talks about all our personal disagreements to her friends. She really embarrasses me sometimes."

Rani was quick to reply, "Bhante, he doesn't respect me, and he scolds me in front of the children. He even ridicules me to my face."

"Calm down, Rani, and you too, Kumara. Never forget that Visakha's father also said to her, 'Never bring fire from inside the home to the outside. Also, never bring fire from outside the home to the inside.' This means that you should keep your quarrels private—and don't bring gossip into the home. Remember these words and you'll eliminate many of your personal problems.

"Furthermore, the Buddha advised, 'Let none find fault in others. Let none see the omissions and commissions of others. But let one see one's own acts done and undone.'[5]

"When speaking to one another, be gentle (*nela*), and use loving words (*premaniya*). Also, remember to use words that are soothing to the ear (*kannasukkha*), and never forget to speak from the heart (*hadhayangama*). Do you think you both can remember to speak to one another this way?" I asked.

Kumara answered, "I'm certainly willing to give it my best." Rani nodded in agreement.

"I believe that a lack of mutual respect for each other causes most of a couple's problems. And the last thing I want to tell you today is the importance of appreciating each other. The Buddha himself said that gifts should be exchanged on a routine basis between husband and wife. He said that these gifts were reminders of the appreciation and respect each one felt for the other. The gifts need not be expensive, but can be simple tokens. Even a single rose from your garden will do."

I am glad to say that in Sri Lanka today, some of the Buddhist temples are performing wedding ceremonies. In America, too, there is no longer controversy over Buddhist weddings for the Sri Lankan community. In fact, after the first wedding for Amali and Reshan, I was soon asked to perform two more ceremonies for Sri Lankan couples.

Now that the tradition of Theravada Buddhist weddings has been established, when couples ask me to perform their wedding ceremonies, I have our *bodicaris*, ordained Buddhist ministers, here at the temple perform them. I have trained the *bodicaris* carefully in this regard, and they carry out their duties beautifully.

Pleasant is life for the couple
Living happily within the Dhamma;
Self-controlled, their words gentle and loving.

Equal in goodness,
Beyond the reach of any foes
They receive the blessings they desire.[6]

◆ ◆ ◆ ◆ ◆ ◆

19 • Solutions to Conflicts

On January 17, 2004, I participated in a symposium at the Baha'i Center in Los Angeles to discuss the topic "Religion as a Dynamic Force in a Changing World." Religious leaders representing the Jewish, Christian, Hindu, Islamic, Baha'i, and Buddhist faiths participated. In Los Angeles this type of discussion is often held at various venues, and there are several local interfaith organizations that sponsor them. Conferences like these help each of the participants understand and respect one another better, and they spotlight our shared beliefs so we can work together to promote peace within our community.

Those of us on the panel that day were asked to deliver a short talk on the topic and then to answer questions. In my own presentation to the symposium, I explained that throughout history, religion has been a dynamic force that has been used by individuals and groups to change the world according to their belief systems. These world changes instigated by religious beliefs have not always been viewed as positive—either at the time or through the lens of history. This is not necessarily because there was any fault in the religions themselves. The fault resided in the fact that the individuals involved acted according to their interpretation of the religion—not necessarily adhering to the inspired truths originally imparted by the religion's founder. It is these interpretations, usually connected to a bid for political power, that have caused so many conflicts and problems. It is these conflicts and problems that have resulted in creating societal separation and divisiveness rather than societal unity and harmony.

The basic underlying moral teachings of all religions are instructions to do good, to avoid evil, and to purify one's self. So, if all of our religious traditions are based on these three common teachings, I asked, why has the world become such a negative place?

The negativity we witness every day—in every corner of the world—results from what the Buddha termed the four causes of bad actions. These are bias, anger, fear and delusion.[1]

Bias is attachment to our own particular perspective of the world, whether it is religious, cultural, social, or political.

Anger is a self-destructive force because it causes us to go blind. When we are angry, we can't see anything with clarity.

Fear so distorts the mind that something or someone perfectly harmless can be viewed as a threat. Fear also causes one to act prematurely, before clearly seeing the truth.

Delusion arises as the result of ignorance, causing us to make decisions based on our personal preferences rather than the facts.

I suggested that we, as the leaders of our respective religious communities, should dedicate ourselves to teaching our congregations how to respect one another's Truth. Recognizing that each of our traditions has its own perspective on what we call "the truth," we need to be careful not to teach that our perspective is the *only* correct perspective, a narrow view that can only cause conflict and separation from others. We need to teach that no single religion has a monopoly on truth; it can be found in all religions.

I offered a quotation from the great Buddhist emperor Asoka, who reigned in India during the third century B.C.E.: "One should not honor only one's own religion and condemn the religions of others. He who thinks he is honoring his own religion by condemning another's religion is deluded. In actual fact, he is harming his own religion. Please be willing to listen to the doctrines professed by others."[2]

I concluded my presentation with the following: "Let us all aim toward creating a world where peace, calm and understanding can prevail. Let wisdom and compassion be the driving forces of all our actions. Let all living beings be treated with fairness and respect, and let peace and harmony reign in our hearts."

After people on the panel had given their talks, the moderator continued the day's discussion by asking the panel what they thought about "nationalism" versus "world government." In my answer I made note that three days after the RMS *Lusitania* was sunk by the Germans in 1915, killing 1,198 people, one of our greatest presidents, Woodrow Wilson, said in an address to a hall filled with newly naturalized citizens of the United States, "My urgent advice to you would be, not only always to think first of America, but always, also, to think first of humanity. You do not love humanity if you seek to divide humanity into jealous camps. Humanity can be welded together only by love, by sympathy, by justice, not by jealousy and hatred."

I then went on to say that Wilson was "the greatest" U.S. president because he had kept us from getting into World War I for as long as possible. It was then that an African American historian on the panel said, "Woodrow Wilson was a complicated man. He was a racist, and that is an undisputed fact. But he also had this great vision for a League of Nations. How could this be in the same person? But it was."

I did not know this fact about Woodrow Wilson, and when I returned to the temple, it dawned on me that the Buddha taught us in the Majjhima Nikaya that conflict arises due to many reasons, and one of them is excessively praising someone. I was embarrassed as I realized that I had made a mistake in saying that Woodrow Wilson was the greatest president. It taught me a lesson: that I should mind my words and remember the Buddha's teachings.

My recent experience at the Baha'i center brought to mind the Aranavibhanga Sutta in which the Buddha taught about the causes of conflict. I reread the sutta and decided to discuss with my Dhamma brothers the importance of having the ability to avoid conflict.

Not creating conflict with others or within oneself is a cardinal principle of Buddhism. Getting caught up in conflict is like being caught up in a web, and escaping from it is difficult without knowing its causes. In the Aranavibhanga Sutta the Buddha explains the five main causes of conflict.

First: *Thinking only of satisfying our own desires can cause conflict.* In Buddhism, if we don't keep a careful watch on our desires, we are likely to cause ourselves suffering.

Second: *Inflicting physical, mental, or emotional harm on one's self can cause conflict.* If we do harm to ourselves for whatever reason, we suffer and those who care about us suffer, thus causing conflict.

Third: *Excessively praising or finding fault with others can cause conflict.* Sibling rivalry is a prime example of the conflict that excessive praise or blame can cause.

Fourth: *Thinking that only your way of thinking, speaking, or acting is right can cause conflict.* No one has a monopoly on being right.

Fifth: *Speaking in harsh tones can cause conflict.* We should always take into consideration how the person we are speaking to might take what we are saying and interpret the tone we are using as an attack on them.

If we have conflict in our lives we can examine our thoughts and actions to see how we may be causing the conflict. The Buddha taught two ideas that will help us to avoid conflict: 1) Thinking before speaking, and 2) knowing happiness, peace, and contentment are found within ourselves.

The first idea relates to Right Speech found in the Eightfold Path. *Right Speech* means speaking truly, speaking correctly, speaking at the appropriate time, and speaking for the benefit of all in a calm and gentle manner. We need to learn self-control in regards to our speech because words are almost always the beginning of any conflict.

Then by knowing happiness, peace, and contentment are found within ourselves, we are able to promote harmony. When we ourselves are happy and peaceful, we do not cause conflict and thereby allow others to become happy and peaceful as well.

Following the principles from the Aranavibhanga Sutta of being mindful of our thoughts and controlling our speech, we can go a long way toward preventing conflict and promoting peace. Thinking back about the incident at the Baha'i center, I told my Dhamma brothers that I should not have become embarrassed by the learned lady's comment about Woodrow Wilson. I clearly made a mistake by using excessive praise. Actually, I owe her a debt of gratitude for giving me the opportunity to reread this particular sutta of the Buddha.

> Be watchful of your words.
> Be watchful of your thoughts,
>> Thus gaining control of your mind.
> Be watchful of your deeds,
>> Thus not committing harm.
> By purifying these three modes of activity,
> Achieve the path of the Great Sage.[3]

♦ ♦ ♦ ♦ ♦ ♦

20 ◆ Rebirth

It is my habit to read the Sri Lankan newspapers on the internet every day, and I am happy I did not miss seeing an article in the September 28, 2006 edition of the Sinhalese newspaper *Divaina*. It was about a fourteen-year-old Sinhalese boy named Aravinda Rupasinghe who one day unexpectedly started speaking in the Tamil language. He not only started speaking in another language, but he completely forgot his real identity and claimed that he was a Tamil girl who lived up north in Jaffna. The story offered a fascinating look at the nature of rebirth.

Aravinda had abruptly announced at school, "My father is a supporter of LTTE"—using the acronym for the Liberation Tamil Tiger Elam, a rebel faction that has been waging war with the government of Sri Lanka since 1983. Over sixty-five thousand people have been killed in this violent campaign to create a separate Tamil state, and everyone in the country is wary of the new strategies LTTE continues to adopt—including boys disguising themselves as girls and girls disguising themselves as boys, as a method of undertaking suicide bombings.

When the principal of Aravinda's school heard this remark he discovered that the boy had only been enrolled in the school for two months. Very little was known about the boy, and he had kept to himself since he came to the school, making very few friends among the other students. It was only natural that the principal would be suspicious of the young man, because suspicion has become a way of life in Sri Lanka; it was indeed very plausible that Aravinda could actually have been a terrorist recruit. The principal contacted the local police station, particularly concerned because of Aravinda's ability to speak Tamil in the Jaffna dialect—Jaffna being a predominantly Tamil area.

The police took Aravinda to the police station and checked his identity papers. They found out who his parents were and dispatched an officer to go to their home and bring them to the station.

"Are you Aravinda's father?" the police officer asked Anura Rupasinghe, a Sinhalese man who lived in a predominately Sinhalese area.

"Yes, of course I am his father. Who says otherwise?" replied Anura.

Without answering, the policeman asked Nandanie, a Sinhalese woman who was Anura's wife, "Are you Aravinda's mother?"

"Yes, I am the boy's natural mother," she replied, distressed.

The policeman turned to the boy, "Are these people your mother and father, Aravinda?"

"No, sir, this woman is my auntie and this man is my uncle. My mother's name is Rasaki Kumar and my father is Ramachandian Ramesh Kumar," he replied. Aravinda's mother began to cry when she heard her son deny that she was his mother.

The policeman still had his doubts and he asked the mother, "Did you adopt a Tamil child?"

Nandanie answered, "No, never. This boy is my own child and he has never spoken Tamil in his life. He has never been to Jaffna, and I am not his aunt. I am his mother."

"How does he know Tamil so well—even the Jaffna dialect?" asked the policeman.

Anura said, "I have no idea where he got this. We do not know how to speak Tamil, we have no relations in Jaffna, and no connections with Tamil people in the north. This is impossible. Until yesterday Aravinda was a normal Sinhalese boy that we have raised since birth."

Aravinda spoke up and said, "I am not a Sinhalese boy—I am

a Tamil girl named Rajee Kumar. This is my aunt and uncle—not my parents. They are wonderful people and they have always cared for me very well."

After the police conducted an extensive investigation they discovered that the parents were telling the truth, and Aravinda was really their son. The family was, in fact, Sinhalese, and they had no knowledge whatsoever of the Tamil language. They also had no connections with Tamil people in the north.

After a few days of counseling and therapy Aravinda finally came to accept his Sinhalese identity and to understand that Rajee, the Tamil girl, was someone who had died in Jaffna and whose life he had lived in a previous birth.

At Dhamma discussion I shared this story with my friends, pointing out how it demonstrates that we can be reborn into any religion, any race, or in any country; we do not have to be reborn as we are in our present life. The Buddha mentioned that samsara's beginning could not be calculated, that beings continually wander from lifetime to lifetime, and that everyone at different times has been our parents, siblings, or children![1]

Grace was the first to question me. "Bhante," she said, "I have read books on the doctrine of rebirth. But how can we prove rebirth is real?"

Buddhists believe in rebirth because the Buddha gave us this knowledge when he explained the cycle of samsara. There is evidence that every individual has lived many lives in the past and will continue to live many lives in the future until he or she attains Nibbana. Advanced meditators oftentimes gain great powers of concentration and are able to recall their previous lives. Hypnotists can also sometimes discover a client's previous lives. Sometimes when a person dies suddenly (*upachchedaka*) and is reborn, their memory of the last lifetime can be recalled before they reach adulthood. A young person's mind is normally pure and unpolluted; therefore the imprint from the trauma of the sudden death makes it a strong memory that is carried over. I explained all this, and then welcomed another question.

"Bhante, was the Buddha able to recall his previous lives?" asked Victor.

I responded that the Buddha was able to view his past lives on the night of his enlightenment. He also saw sentient beings dying in one state of existence, and being reborn in another—according to their actions. Therefore, it was from personal experience that the Buddha taught his followers the truth of rebirth. The Buddha had six supernormal psychic abilities,[2] I explained further. These abilities are 1) magical powers (*iddhividha*), 2) divine ear (*dibba sota*), 3) telepathy or mind-reading (*ceto pariyanana*), 4) remembrance of past lives (*pubbenivasanussati*), 5) divine eye (*dibba cakkhu*), and 6) destruction of mental pollutants (*assavakhaya*). I said the fourth ability includes being able to see other peoples' past lives as well as his own. The Buddha used this knowledge to help his followers understand themselves.

I continued by telling the group that in recent years, more and more evidence has been collected and documented that supports the idea of rebirth. Professor Ian Stevenson of the University of Virginia has researched and published his discoveries in over twenty cases of rebirth.[3] These cases that have been verified are from various countries including France, Italy, Burma, Sri Lanka, and India. I recommended that my friends who might be interested should read a spellbinding book by Brian Weiss titled *Many Lives, Many Masters*.

"Dr. Weiss uses hypnosis to engage his clients in past life regression," I continued. "I am sure this book will answer most of your questions."

"I'm really confused, Bhante. Are rebirth and reincarnation the same thing?" Victor asked.

"Some believe that rebirth and reincarnation are the same," I said, "but actually, they are not. They have completely different philosophical meanings depending on the religion. The word rein-carnation (*punaruthpathi*) is associated with Hinduism, where it is believed that when a person dies, the soul goes in search of a suitable person and place in which to be reborn. According to the Bhagavad Gita the soul does not die and it cannot be destroyed. The soul is reincarnated." I recited the following passage:

Being at the beginning,
Not born nor dying,
It cannot be said
One comes to be,
And will be no more.
Not changing,
One will be everlasting
Even though the body may be slain.[4]

"In Buddhism, we believe in rebirth, or *punabbhava*, which means 'again becoming.' The Buddha said that for a birth to take place, three conditions must be present at conception: the parent's fertility, sexual union, and the development of the new being. When a person dies, his or her mental energy (kamma) estab-lishes itself in a new state of being. The new individual grows, and a new personality develops that is influenced by the mental char-acteristics that he or she carried over from his or her previous life. We have to remember that mind and matter are always changing.

"There are two types of existences in this world. One has a mind and a consciousness; the other has a life but no conscious-ness. A human being is made up of both mind and body. Both of these are always changing; thoughts arise and fade away, the cells in the body are continually being replaced—all in the wink of an eye.

"For example, when we see a lighted candle we perceive only one flame. In actuality, however, every instant the candle burns there is a new flame. Life is like that, too. Every moment we are being born and we die."

Victor asked, "After I die, will I transmigrate to another body?"

I replied, "King Milinda asked Venerable Nagasena that same question: 'Is there any being that transmigrates from this body to another?'

"Venerable Nagasena replied, 'No, there is not.'

"'If that is so, would there be an escape from the result of evil deeds?' asked the king.

"Venerable Nagasena answered, 'Yes, there would be an escape if they were *not* to be reborn, but there would not be an escape if they *were* to be reborn. The mind and body process we refer to as a human being performs deeds that are either pure or impure, which creates kamma. Because of this kamma another mind and body process is born. Therefore, the new mind and body (human being) is *not* free from its evil deeds.'

"'Give me an example,' demanded the king.

"'If a thief were to steal another man's mangoes, would he deserve punishment?' asked Venerable Nagasena.

"'Indeed he would,' replied the king.

"'But the mangoes he stole were not the same ones that the owner originally planted. The ones he stole were from the *tree* that grew from the mangoes that were originally planted. Why should he deserve punishment?' Venerable Nagasena asked the king.

"'Because the mangoes he stole were the result of the *seeds* of the mango that the owner originally planted,' answered the king.

"'Just so, O king,' Venerable Nasagena continued. 'This human being, or mind and body process, commits deeds that are either pure or impure, and because of that new kamma, another mind and body process is reborn. Thus the new mind and body process is *not free* from its evil deeds.'"[5]

Chintana then asked me another question. "Bhante, my husband is a very loving, caring man. Is it possible for me to have him as my husband in my next life?"

"Yes, Chintana, rebirth gives us an opportunity to perfect the skills and interests we have developed in this life. The Buddha said that we may even meet the people we love in our next life if we have a strong attachment or desire for each other. Let me illustrate this with a story from the Buddha's time.

"A virtuous couple named Nakulamata, the wife, and Nakulapita, the husband, paid the Buddha a visit. Nakulapita said that during his marriage of over forty years he never had an unkind thought about his wife, and he desired to have her as his wife in his next life. His wife repeated the same things about her husband, and she expressed her desire to be his wife in their next life. The Buddha replied, 'If both husband and wife desire to behold each other in both this life and the next life, and both are matched in faith, matched in virtue, matched in generosity, and matched in wisdom, then they will behold each other in both this life and the next life also.'"

As a final word, I reminded the group that the Buddha declared that it was the force of their kamma that caused people to be born and reborn endlessly. When one follows the Noble Eightfold Path taught by the Buddha, eventually one attains Nibbana and the cycle stops.

> Thru many births have I wandered in samsara,
> Vainly seeking the builder of this house.
> Sorrowful is repeated births.
> O house builder, I see you!
> You shall not build this house again!
> All your rafters are broken and
>   your ridgepole shattered!
> My mind has ceased building and craving.[6]

◆ ◆ ◆ ◆ ◆ ◆

NOTES

The following endnotes include information to help the reader locate suttas that are mentioned in the text, for those who wish to read further. Verse numbers from the Dhammapada are given in the endnote. Many translations of the Dhammapada have been made throughout the years. The ones in this book are not word-for-word translations from the Pali but rather are freestyle interpretations by the author in an effort to convey the essence of the verse for today's reader.

Over the centuries many stories have been told to illustrate the teachings of the Buddha. Some of the stories were told by the Buddha as a teaching tool. Other stories are found in the various commentaries that were written about the different collections (*nikayas*) of the suttas and the collection of sayings known as the Dhammapada. Learning these stories is part of the training a monk receives. Monks in turn retell these ancient stories to help those who come to them for help.

1 ◆ Dealing with Anger

1. Venerable Narada, *The Buddha & His Teachings* (Colombo, Sri Lanka: Lever Brothers Cultural Conservation Trust, 1987), p. 380.

2. "Maharahulavada Sutta," in the Majjhima Nikaya.

3. Walpola Piyananda, *Love in Buddhism* (Los Angeles: Dharma Vijaya Buddhist Vihara, 1990), p. 38.

4. Venerable B. Ananda Maitreya Thera, *Development of the Divine States* (Los Angeles: Dharma Vijaya Buddhist Vihara, 1988), p. 14.

5. Walpola Piyananda, *Love in Buddhism*, pp. 41–42.

6. Ibid., p. 2.

7. Verse 36, Vasettha Sutta, in the Sutta Nipata.

2 ✦ Imagination and Reality

1. Verse 227, Dhammapada. The story about Atula can be found in the commentary on the Dhammapada.

2. Verse 81, Dhammapada.

3. The story of Socrates' Three Filters appears in numerous sources, but its actual author is unknown.

4. Verse 50, in the Sutta Nipata.

3 ✦ Bamiyan Buddha Statues

1. Verse 5, Dhammapada.

2. "Culakammavibhanga Sutta," in the Majjhima Nikaya.

3. Nyanatiloka, "Kamma," in *Buddhist Dictionary*, 4th ed. (Kandy, Sri Lanka: Buddhist Publication Society, 1970), pp. 77–78.

4. Verses 318–319, Dhammapada.

4 ✦ Food for Thought

1. Bhante H. Gunaratana Maha Thera, "Mindful Eating," *Bhavana Newsletter* 7, no. 2 (April–June 1991), p. 5.

2. "Dhammacakkapavattana Sutta," in the Samyutta Nikaya.

3. Section 3, Kosalasamyutta II, in the Samyutta Nikaya.

4. Bhante H. Gunaratana Maha Thera, "Mindful Eating."

5. "Vitakkhansanthana Sutta," in the Majjhima Nikaya.

6. "Salayatana Samyutta," in the Samyutta Nikaya.

5 ✦ Four Factors for Life

1. "Ratana Sutta," in the Sutta Nipata.

2. Bhikkhu Nanamoli, trans., *The Path of Purification: Visuddhimagga* (Taipei, Taiwan: Corporate Body of the Buddha Educational Foundation, 2003), p. 420.

3. Ibid, p. 422.

4. Moni Bagchee, *Our Buddha* (Kuala Lumpur, Malayasia, Buddhist Missionary Society, 1999), p. 47.

5. "Kalama Sutta," in the Anguttara Nikaya.

6 ◆ Are Buddhists Idol Worshippers?

1. Verse 2, Dhammapada.

2. "Alagaddupanna Sutta," in the Majjhima Nikaya.

3. Moni Bagchee, *Our Buddha* (Kuala Lumpur, Malaysia: Buddhist Missionary Society, 1999), p. 47.

4. "Sangiti Sutta," in the Digha Nikaya.

5. Buddha Vandana, *A Book of Buddhist Devotions* (Los Angeles: Dharma Vijaya Buddhist Vihara, 1990), p. 4.

6. Anjana Gamage, "Image of Buddha Even Inspired Nehru," *Sunday Observer*, October 19, 2003.

7. Verses 206–208, Dhammapada.

7 ◆ A Catastrophe

1. Mahathera Ledi Saydaw, "Niyama," in *The Manuals of Buddhism* (Rangoon, Burma: Union Buddha Sasana Council, 1965), pp. 103–36.

2. "Vasettha Sutta," in the Sutta Nipata.

3. Verses 1–2, Dhammapada.

4. Sharm De Alwis, "Saved by a Crocodile," *Daily News* (Sri Lanka), January 11, 2005.

5. "Sagathavagga I," in the Samyutta Nikaya.

8 ◆ Power of Meditation

1. "Book of Ones," in the Samyutta Nikaya.

2. "Ariyapariyesana Sutta," in the Majjhima Nikaya.

3. "Satipattana Sutta," in the Majjhima Nikaya.

4. "Girimananda Sutta," in the Anguttara Nikaya.

5. Bahiya, in the Udana.

6. "Bhaddekaratta Sutta," in the Majjhima Nikaya.

9 ◆ Getting to Know You, America

1. Verse 5, Dhammapada.

2. The Bible, Book of Matthew 5:38–48.

3. Verse 223, Dhammapada.

4. "Book of Fours," F. L. Woodward, trans. *The Gradual Sayings*, vol. 2 (London: Pali Text Society, 1982), p. 186.

10 ◆ The Meditator

1. "Book of Sixes," E. M. Hare, trans., *The Gradual Sayings*, vol. 3 (London: Pali Text Society, 1973), p. 252.

2. "Meghiya Sutta," Book of Nines, in the Anguttara Nikaya.

3. Meghiya, also found in the Udana.

11 ◆ Spiritual Friends

1. "The Half," Maggasamyutta of the Samyutta Nikaya.

2. Ibid.

3. "Book of Nines," in the Anguttara Nikaya.

4. Walpola Piyananda, *Buddhist Ministry in the West* (Los Angeles: Dharma Vijaya Buddhist Vihara, 2005), pp. 39–40.

5. Bhikkhu Nanamoli, trans., *Path of Purification: Visuddhimagga* (Taipei, Taiwan: Corporate Body of the Buddha Educational Foundation, 2003), p. 24.

6. Verse 328–330, Dhammapada.

12 ◆ Virtue

1. "Bhaddali Sutta," in the Majjhima Nikaya.

2. Bhikkhu Nanamoli, trans., *The Path of Purification: Vissuddhimagga* (Taipei, Taiwan: Corporate Body of the Buddha Educational Foundation, 2005), p. 3.

3. "Sangati Sutta," in the Digha Nikaya.
4. Verses 1–2, Dhammapada.
5. "Ambalattika Rahulovada Sutta," in the Majjhima Nikaya.
6. Verse 183, Dhammapada.
7. Verse 368, Dhammapada.

13 ◆ Mistaken Identity

1. "Kalama Sutta," in the Anguttara Nikaya.
2. Verse 43, Dhammapada.
3. Verses 3–4, Dhammapada.

14 ◆ Overcoming Gambling

1. "Sigalovada Sutta," in *Ten Suttas from the Digha Nikaya* (Rangoon, Burma: Pitaka Association, 1984), p. 436.
2. "Dvedhavitakka Sutta," in the Majjhima Nikaya.
3. "Vitakkasanthana Sutta," in the Majjhima Nikaya.
4. Verse 172, Dhammapada.

15 ◆ Dealing with Death

1. "Salla Sutta," in the Sutta Nipata.
2. Weragoda Sarada Maha Thera, trans., "Kisa Gotami Story," in *Treasury of Truth: Illustrated Dhammapada* (Taipei, Taiwan: Buddha Educational Foundation), p. 243.
3. Narada Maha Thera, trans., *A Manual of Abhidhamma* (Singapore: Buddhist Meditation Centre, 1989), pp. 270–271.
4. Verse 128, Dhammapada.

16 ◆ Music and Chanting in Buddhism

1. "Sona Sutta," Anguttara Nikaya.
2. "Sakkapanna Sutta," Digha Nikaya.
3. Verse 268, Dhammapada.

17 • The Bhikkhuni Order

1. I. B. Horner, trans., "Cullavagga X," in *Vinaya: The Book of the Discipline* (London: Pali Text Society, 1975), p. 353.

2. Ibid., p. 357.

3. Ibid., p. 354.

4. "Mahaparinibbana Sutta," in *Ten Suttas from Digha Nikaya: Long Discourses of the Buddha* (Rangoon, Burma: Pitaka Association, 1984), p. 269.

5. Verse 195, Dhammapada.

6. "Brahmajala Sutta," in the Digha Nikaya.

7. Verse 10, Dhammapada.

18 • Marriage Ceremonies

1. "Book of Eights," section 49, in *The Book of Gradual Sayings*, vol. 5. E. M. Hare, trans., (London: Pali Text Society, 1978), pp. 178–179.

2. "Sigalovada Sutta," in *Ten Suttas from the Digha Nikaya* (Rangoon, Burma: Burma Pitaka Association, 1984), p. 443.

3. Ibid.

4. "Book of Eights," section 49, in *The Book of Gradual Sayings*, vol. 5, pp. 178–179.

5. Verse 50, Dhammapada.

6. "Book of Fours," in *The Book of Gradual Sayings* (London: Pali Text Society, 1982), p. 70.

19 • Solutions to Conflicts

1. Sigalovada Sutta, in the Digha Nikaya.

2. Asoka rock edict XII. Emperor Asoka carved edicts on rocks throughout his empire as guiding principles for his people.

3. Verse 281, Dhammapada.

20 • Rebirth

1. Mrs. Rhys Davids, "Nidanavagga," chapter 15, in *The Book of the Kindred Sayings II* (London: Pali Text Society, 1952), p. 128.

2. "Dasuttara Sutta," in the Digha Nikaya.

3. Ian Stevenson, M.D., *Twenty Cases Suggestive of Reincarnation* (Charlottesville: University Press of Virginia, 1974).

4. The Bhagavad Gita, chapter 2, verse 20.

5. N. K. G. Mendis, trans., *The Questions of King Milinda* (Kandy, Sri Lanka: Buddhist Publication Society, 1993), p. 44.

6. Verse 153–154, Dhammapada.

GLOSSARY

The words in italics listed below are Pali, except where indicated.

anagārika	One who leaves home to practice Buddhism, but does not become a monk.
ānāpanasati	Mindfulness of in-and-out breathing; a form of meditation.
anatta	Doctrine of the nonexistence of a permanent, unchanging ego entity (soul).
anicca	Impermanence.
anurakkhana	One of the "four right efforts"; the effort to maintain or preserve.
arahat	A "worthy one." One who has eliminated all defilements (lust, anger, and ignorance) and attained full liberation.
ārakkha-sampadā	The principle that one should protect one's income.
āsavakhaya ñana	One who has the wisdom to destroy one's defilements.
aṭṭhangasīla	Observance of the Eight Precepts (*see below*) by lay people, on full moon days or during retreats.
āyukkhaya	Death by natural causes in old age.
Bhagavad Gitā	(Sanskrit). Highly revered Hindu religious book; the dialogue between Arjuna and Krishna.

bhaya	Fear.
bhikkhu	Fully ordained Buddhist monk.
bhikkhuni	Fully ordained Buddhist nun.
Buddha Gaya	(Bodhgaya) The place where the Buddha attained enlightenment.
cāritta sīla	Moral activities that should be performed.
ceto pariyayañana	Ability to read the minds of others.
chanda	A strong intention: 1. In *iddhipada, chanda* is for good. 2. In *agati, chanda* is for bad.
citta	Mind. The mind, however, has three functioning parts: vinnana, mano, and citta.
dāna	Generosity. In the Theravada tradition it is the offering of food to monks or nuns.
Dhamma	Buddha's teachings.
dibba cakku	Clairvoyance.
dibba sōta	Clairaudience.
dōsa	Anger.
Eight Precepts	Rules for behavior observed by laypeople on full moon days and at meditation retreats, as follows: 1. I undertake the precept to abstain from killing; 2. I undertake the precept to abstain from stealing; 3. I undertake the precept to practice celibacy; 4. I undertake the precept to abstain from lying; 5. I undertake the precept to abstain from alcohol and drugs that cause heedlessness; 6. I undertake the precept to abstain from eating at improper times; 7. I undertake the precept to abstain from dancing, singing, music, shows,

	wearing garlands, using perfumes, and beautifying myself with cosmetics; 8. I undertake the precept to abstain from the use of high and large seats and beds.
Five Precepts	Rules for behavior observed by Buddhists, as follows: 1. I undertake the precept to abstain from killing; 2. I undertake the precept to abstain from stealing; 3. I undertake the precept to abstain from sexual misconduct; 4. I undertake the precept to abstain from lying; 5. I undertake the precept to abstain from alcohol and drugs that cause heedlessness.
Gandhāra	The Kingdom of Gandhara lasted from the sixth century B.C.E. to the eleventh century C.E. and was at its peak during the reign of Buddhist Kushan kings; it was located in what today is the Valley of Peshaavar in Pakistan.
hiri	Self respect: that which keeps one from wrong doing thereby avoiding moral shame.
iddhivida	Magical powers.
kalyānamitta	Spiritual friend who leads you along the right path.
kamma	Action, referring to intentional mental, verbal, and bodily behavior; Karma (Sanskrit).
kammakkaya	Karmic energy is used up.
Mahājayamaṅgala Gāthā	Verses of the great joyous victory, usually chanted as a blessing.

Mahāyāna	"Great vehicle," tradition of Buddhism developed seven hundred years after the Buddha, mainly practiced in China, Korea, and Japan; the main sects include Pure Land, Zen, and Tantric.
manō	Intellect.
Manu	(Sanskrit). In Hinduism, progenitor of humankind, the first king to rule the earth.
manussa	Refers to the mind of a human being.
mettā	Loving-kindness, universal love.
Milinda	King of the city of Sagala in India (189–167 B.C.E.).
mōha	Ignorance.
Okyo	(Japanese). The Japanese term for sutta; *o*, is an honorific and *kyo* means "sutta."
ottappa	Moral dread.
Pañcasikha	Musician for Sakka, king of the thirty-three gods.
pañcasīla	The Five Precepts (*see above*) normally observed by lay Buddhists every day.
paññā	Wisdom.
pirith	(Sinhala). The chanting of suttas for blessing and protection.
pubbenivāsānussati	Remembrance of former lives.
punabbhava	Rebirth.
punaruthpati	(Sanskrit). In Hinduism, reincarnation.
roshi	(Japanese). Literally "old [venerable] master"; a title in Zen; this teacher can be male or female.

saddhā	Faith, belief, or confidence.
sake	Japanese wine made from rice.
Sakka	King of the heaven of the thirty-three gods.
samādhi	Concentration or mental discipline.
samajīvikatā	The principle of living within one's income.
sāmanēra	Novice Buddhist monk.
sāmanēri	Novice Buddhist nun.
samsara	The round of rebirths without a discoverable beginning.
Sangha	Community of Buddhist clergy, both male and female.
sayadaw	Teacher; Burmese title for a Buddhist monk.
sīla	Virtue, morality.
Sinhala	Indo-Aryan language spoken in Sri Lanka.
Tamil	Dravidian language primarily spoken in southern India and northern Sri Lanka.
Theravada	"The way of the elders," the tradition considered to be the oldest and most authentic of the Buddha's teachings.
Tripitaka	"Three baskets," referring to the three main canonical divisions of the Buddha's teaching into 1. the Buddha's discourses (suttas); 2. the code of monastic discipline (Vinaya); and 3. philosophy (*abhidhamma*).
ubhayakkhaya	Death from old age when karmic force is finished.
upacchedaka	Sudden death caused by an outside source.

upāsaka	A male Buddhist who is not a monk and who keeps the Five Precepts.
upāsikā	A female Buddhist who is not a nun and who keeps the Five Precepts.
utthānasampadā	Efficiency, energy.
Vajrayāna	"Diamond Vehicle," Tibetan Buddhist tradition.
vāritta sila	Moral practice of avoidance; such as following the the Five Precepts.
viññāna	Consciousness or perception.
viriya	Application of energy.
zazen	(Japanese). Literally, *za*, "sitting," and *Zen*, "absorption"; meditative practice taught in Zen.

ABOUT THE AUTHOR

Venerable Walpola Piyananda, "Bhante," is the founder, president and abbot of Dharma Vijaya Buddhist Vihara in Los Angeles, California. Bhante was born in 1943 in the village of Walpola. Following the Sri Lankan tradition, he was ordained as a novice monk at the age of twelve. He gave up his given lay and family names, and took his village name Walpola and was also given the Buddhist name Piyananda, meaning "pleasant joy." He was no longer just a member of his biological family, but now the entire village was his family, the broadest level of organization in the traditional Buddhist society. Bhante was fully ordained in 1970.

Bhante was a part-time teacher at the Sri Lanka College in Maradana from 1964 until 1969. He attended Kelaniya University from 1963 to 1967. At the university, Bhante was the leader of the debate team. He won first place in the 1966 Inter-University Oratorical Contest sponsored by the Indian Embassy in Sri Lanka. Bhante graduated with Honors with a BA in Buddhist Studies from Kelaniya University. In 1969 he joined the faculty at Vidyodaya University as an assistant lecturer and also became a member of the faculty at Colombo University as a visiting lecturer. He taught at both these universities until the end of 1972 when he resigned to continue his studies abroad.

Bhante had been awarded a Commonwealth Scholarship by the Indian government, which allowed him to study abroad. He left Sri Lanka for the first time and went to study Pali and Hinduism at the Calcutta University in India, where he earned a MA in Pali. While studying in Calcutta, Bhante worked with Mother Teresa and helped with Buddhist activities at the Maha Bodhi Society.

Bhante is one of the founding members and is the current president of the Buddhist Sangha Council of Southern California. He is also the Chief Sangha Nayaka Thera in America (leader of his denomination). He serves as advisor to the president of Sri Lanka on international religious affairs. He has provided many services for Southeast Asian refuges in L.A., and was Buddhist chaplain for the 1984 Los Angeles Olympic Games. He currently teaches Dhamma and meditation at his temple in Los Angeles, Dharma Vijaya Buddhist Vihara, one of the oldest Theravada temples in the United States.

A frequent speaker on Buddhist issues in the United States and around the world, Bhante is also the author of numerous articles and books in English and his native Sinhala. In 2001 he published *Saffron Days in L.A.: Tales of a Buddhist Monk in America*. *The Bodhi Tree Grows in L.A.* is a sequel to that work.